Seattle Mariners 2019

A Baseball Companion

Edited by Patrick Dubuque, Aaron Gleeman and Bret Sayre

Baseball Prospectus

Craig Brown and Dave Pease, Consultant Editors
Rob McQuown and Harry Pavlidis, Statistics Editors

Copyright © 2019 by DIY Baseball, LLC.
All rights reserved

This book or any part thereof may not be reproduced or transmitted in any form or by any means, electronic or mechanical, including photocopying, recording, or by any information storage and retrieval system, without permission in writing from the publisher.

Limit of Liability/Disclaimer of Warranty: While the publisher and the author have used their best efforts in preparing this book, they make no representations or warranties with respect to the accuracy or completeness of the contents of this book and specifically disclaim any implied warranties of merchantability or fitness for a particular purpose. No warranty may be created or extended by sales representatives or written sales materials. The advice and strategies contained herein may not be suitable for your situation. You should consult with a professional where appropriate. Neither the publisher nor the author shall be liable for any loss of profit or any other commercial damages, including but not limited to special, incidental, consequential, or other damages.

Library of Congress Cataloging-in-Publication Data:
paperback
ISBN-13: 978-1-949332-22-3

Project Credits
Cover Design: Kathleen Dyson
Interior Design and Production: Jeff Pease, Dave Pease
Layout: Jeff Pease, Dave Pease

Baseball icon courtesy of Uberux, from https://www.shareicon.net/author/uberux

Ballpark diagram courtesy of Lou Spirito/THIRTY81 Project, https://thirty81project.com/

Manufactured in the United States of America
10 9 8 7 6 5 4 3 2 1

Table of Contents

Foreword v
    Rob Mains

Statistical Introduction vii

Part 1: Team Analysis

Table for Two: Previewing the 2019 Seattle Mariners 3
    Nathan Bishop and Matt Ellis

Performance Graphs 9

2018 Team Performance 10

2019 Team Projections 11

Team Personnel 12

T-Mobile Park Stats 13

Mariners Team Analysis 15

Part 2: Player Analysis

Mariners Player Analysis 20

Mariners Prospects 83

Part 3: Featured Articles

The Hole in The Shift is Fixing Itself 97
    Russell Carleton

The State of the Quality Start 101
    Rob Mains

Heads-Up Hacking—The First Pitch 107
    Matthew Trueblood

A Hymn for the Index Stat 113
    Patrick Dubuque

Index of Names 117

Foreword

Rob Mains

Welcome to this companion of the 2019 Seattle Mariners. We at Baseball Prospectus are excited to provide this analysis of the Mariners.

Our website, Baseball Prospectus, is a leader in delivering high-quality commentary and data to baseball fans everywhere. To some, those words—commentary and data—appear mutually exclusive. There are people out there who believe that traditional analysis and advanced analytics must run on different paths. But the simplistic narrative of stats vs. traditionalists just isn't true. Every team's analytics department interacts with scouting, development, and major league operations with a common goal: Delivering a championship. New technologies, like radar tracking of pitch speeds and movement, enable talent evaluators to focus on qualitative aspects of pitching like mechanics and pitch sequencing. In-game strategies like infield shifts, based on batters' hit tendencies, help turn balls in play into outs. Hitters use information to adjust their swings to maximize run production.

All these numbers can seem, at best, intimidating, and at worst, counterproductive to the casual fan. Even as technology and analysis have embedded themselves deeply into the way teams run, it can often feel like statistics create a displacement between the viewer and the sport, breaking them out of the action. And yet every fan incorporates the numbers to some degree; stats like batting average and earned run average, so fundamental to how we talk about performance, are actually complicated formulas. They don't bother people because those formulas have become second nature, as easy to translate as the action on the field.

Along the way, new statistics have entered baseball's lexicon. You'll see some of them, like on-base percentage (which measures a batter's ability to get on base via walk, hit batter, or hit), OPS (on-base plus slugging), and average exit velocity (the speed of balls off a hitter's bat) on broadcasts. Others, like DRC+, might well be new to you. Some of them have been well-defined to the public, others haven't. That lack of context has created ambiguity. Fans know that a ball hit 100 mph is scorched, but does that mean extra bases? (Not if it's hit on the ground or high in the air it doesn't.)

Seattle Mariners 2019

For those who are amenable to them, the new statistics can increase the enjoyment and understanding of the game. They can help fans identify when a pitcher is tiring, when a stolen base or a bunt attempt makes sense (and, more often, when it doesn't), or how a team's lineup might be constructed. Websites like Baseball Prospectus add to that understanding by weaving metrics into the narrative of the game. That's the goal of this publication: to take some of the newer, more complicated statistics and make them as intuitive as the ones on the back of old baseball cards.

But you don't need to love analytics to love baseball. The fans at BP who worked together to write this guide are captivated first and foremost by the game itself. We're drawn to Aaron Judge's power, Francisco Lindor's glove, Billy Hamilton's speed and Patrick Corbin's slider and don't need numbers to tell us why they're so mesmerizing. The underlying statistics provide depth to the game that we all love.

We hope you'll find that this guide helps you better understand the Mariners. Our analysts have studied the team's major league personnel and its minor league affiliates to identify their strengths and weaknesses, both the obvious ones and those that only a careful dissection of players' performances—yes, including the data—can reveal. You don't need us to tell you who was good and who wasn't in 2018, but our models and writers can help you project how each player is going to perform this year and beyond, and appreciate the greatness of each new game as it unfolds. As in the sport itself, the human and analytic components combine to generate a deeper overall understanding.

Think back to the first time you saw a baseball game on a high-definition TV. You'd grown familiar with how the game looked and felt on a picture tube. But new TV allowed you to see details that you'd never seen before. That's how advanced statistics work. The game itself is why you're here and why you're buying this. (And, for that matter, why we wrote it.) The statistical measures provide the sharper focus, the detail, the depth of knowledge that you didn't have before, generating an overall superior picture. Enjoy the view.

—*Rob Mains is an author of Baseball Prospectus.*

Statistical Introduction

Sports are, fundamentally, a blend of athletic endeavor and storytelling. Baseball, like any other sport, tells its stories in so many ways: in the arc of a game from the stands or a season from the box scores, in photos, or even in numbers. At Baseball Prospectus, we understand that statistics don't replace observation or any of baseball's stories, but complement everything else that makes the game so much fun.

What stats help us with is with patterns and precision, variance and value. This book can help you learn things you may not see from watching a game or hundred, whether it's the path of a career over time or the breadth of the entire MLB. We'd also never ask you to choose between our numbers and the experience of viewing a game from the cheap seats or the comfort of your home; our publication combines running the numbers with observations and wisdom from some of the brightest minds we can find. But if you *do* want to learn more about the numbers beyond what's on the backs of player jerseys, let us help explain.

Offense

At the end of this past year, we've revised our methodology for determining batting value. Long-time readers of Baseball Prospectus will notice that we've retired True Average in favor of a new metric: Deserved Runs Created Plus (DRC+). Developed by Jonathan Judge and our stats team, this statistic measures everything a player does at the plate–reaching base, hitting for power, making outs, and moving runners over–and puts it on a scale where 100 equals league-average performance. A DRC+ of 150 is terrific, a DRC+ of 100 is average, and a DRC+ of 75 means you better be an excellent defender.

DRC+ also does a better job than any of our previous metrics in taking contextual factors into account. The model adjusts for how the park affects performance, but also for things like the talent of the opposing pitcher, value of different types of batted-ball events, league, temperature, and other factors. It's able to describe a player's expected offensive contribution than any other statistic we've found over the years, and also does a better job of predicting future performance as well.

The other aspect of run-scoring is baserunning, which we quantify using Baserunning Runs. BRR not only records the value of stolen bases (or getting caught in the act), but also accounts for a runner's ability to go first to third on a single or advance on a fly ball.

Defense

Where offensive value is *relatively* easy to identify and understand, defensive value is ... not. Over the past dozen years, the sabermetric community has focused mostly on stats based on zone data: a real-live human person records the type of batted ball and estimated landing location, and models are created that give expected outs. From there, you can compare fielders' actual outs to those expected ones. Simple, right?

Unfortunately, zone data has two major issues. First, zone data is recorded by commercial data providers who keep the raw data private unless you pay for it. (All the statistics we build in this book and on our website use public data as inputs.) That hurts our ability to test assumptions or duplicate results. Second, over the years it has become apparent that there's quite a bit of "noise" in zone-based fielding analysis. Sometimes the conclusions drawn from zone data don't hold up to scrutiny, and sometimes the different data provided by different providers don't look anything alike, giving wildly different results. Sometimes the hard-working professional stringers or scorers might unknowingly inflict unconscious bias into the mix: for example good fielders will often be credited with more expected outs despite the data, and ballparks with high press boxes tend to score more line drives than ones with a lower press box.

Enter our Fielding Runs Above Average (FRAA). For most positions, FRAA is built from play-by-play data, which allows us to avoid the subjectivity found in many other fielding metrics. The idea is this: count how many fielding plays are made by a given player and compare that to expected plays for an average fielder at their position (based on pitcher ground-ball tendencies and batter handedness). Then we adjust for park and base-out situations.

When it comes to catchers, our methodology is a little different thanks to the laundry list of responsibilities they're tasked with beyond just, well, catching and throwing the ball. By now you've probably heard about "framing" or the art of making umpires more likely to call balls outside the strike zone for strikes. To put this into one tidy number, we incorporate pitch tracking data (for the years it exists) and adjust for important factors like pitcher, umpire, batter, and home-field advantage using a mixed-model approach. This grants us a number for how many strikes the catcher is personally adding to (or subtracting from) his pitchers' performance ... which we then convert to runs added or lost using linear weights.

Framing is one of the biggest parts of determining catcher value, but we also take into account blocking balls from going past, whether a scorer deems it a passed ball or a wild pitch. We use a similar approach–one that really benefits from the pitch tracking data that tells us what ends up in the dirt and what doesn't. We also include a catcher's ability to prevent stolen bases and how well they field balls in play, and *finally* we come up with our FRAA for catchers.

Pitching

Both pitching and fielding make up the half of baseball that isn't run scoring: run prevention. Separating pitching from fielding is a tough task, and most recent pitching analysis has branched off from Voros McCracken's famous (and controversial) statement, "There is little if any difference among major-league pitchers in their ability to prevent hits on balls hit in the field of play." The research of the analytic community has validated this to some extent, and there are a host of "defense-independent" pitching measures that have been developed to try and extricate the effect of the defense behind a hurler from the pitcher's work.

Our solution to this quandry is Deserved Run Average (DRA), our core pitching metric. DRA looks like earned run average (ERA), the tried-and-true pitching stat you've seen on every baseball broadcast or box score from the past century, but it's very different. To start, DRA takes an event-by-event look at what the pitchers does, and adjusts the value of that event based on different environmental factors like park, batter, catcher, umpire, base-out situation, run differential, inning, defense, home field advantage, pitcher role, and temperature. That mixed model gives us a pitcher's expected contribution, similar to what we do for our DRC+ model for hitters and FRAA model for catchers. (Oh, and we also consider the pitcher's effect on basestealing and on balls getting past the catcher.)

It's important to note that DRA is set to the scale of runs allowed per nine innings (RA9) instead of ERA, which makes DRA's scale slightly higher than ERA's. The reason for this is because ERA tends to overrate three types of pitchers:

1. Pitchers who play in parks where scorers hand out more errors. Official scorers differ significantly in the frequency at which they assign errors to fielders.
2. Ground-ball pitchers, because a substantial proportion of errors occur on grounders.
3. Pitchers who aren't very good. Better pitchers often allow fewer unearned runs than bad pitchers, because good pitchers tend to find ways to get out of jams.

Since the last time you picked up an edition of this book, we've also made a few minor changes to DRA to make it better. Recent research into "tunneling"–the act of throwing consecutive pitches that appear similar from a batter's point of view until after the swing decision point–data has given us a new contextual factor to account for in DRA: plate distance. This refers to the distance between successive pitches as they approach the plate, and while it has a smaller effect than factors like velocity or whiff rate, it still can help explain pitcher strikeout rate in our model.

New Pitching Metrics for 2019

We're including a few "new" pitching metrics for 2019's suite of Baseball Prospectus publications, but you may be familiar with them if you've spent time scouring the internet for stats.

Fastball Percentage

Our fastball percentage (FB%) statistic measures how frequently a pitcher throws a pitch classified as a "fastball," measured as a percentage of overall pitches thrown. We qualify three types of fastballs:

1. The traditional four-seam fastball;
2. The two-seam fastball or sinker;
3. "Hard cutters," which are pitches that have the movement profile of a cut fastball and are used as the pitcher's primary offering or in place of a more traditional fastball.

For example, a pitcher with a FB% of 67 throws any combination of these three pitches about two-thirds of the time.

Whiff Rate

Everybody loves a swing and a miss, and whiff rate (WHF) measures how frequently pitchers induce a swinging strike. To calculate WHF, we add up all the pitches thrown that ended with a swinging strike, then divide that number by a pitcher's total pitches thrown. Most often, high whiff rates correlate with high strikeout rates (and overall effective pitcher performance).

Called Strike Probability

Called Strike Probability (CSP) is a number that represents the likelihood that all of a pitcher's pitches will be called a strike while controlling for location, pitcher and batter handedness, umpire and count. Here's how it works: on each pitch, our model determines how many times (out of 100) that a similar pitch was called for a strike given those factors mentioned above, and when normalized for each batter's strike zone. Then we average the CSP for all pitches thrown by a pitcher in a season, and that gives us the yearly CSP percentage you see in the stats boxes.

As you might imagine, pitchers with a higher CSP are more likely to work in the zone, where pitchers with a lower CSP are likely locating their pitches outside the normal strike zone, for better or for worse.

Projections

Many of you aren't turning to this book just for a look at what a player has done, but for a look at what a player is going to do: the PECOTA projections. PECOTA, initially developed by Nate Silver (who has moved on to greater fame as a political analyst), consists of three parts:

1. Major-league equivalencies, which use minor-league statistics to project how a player will perform in the major leagues;
2. Baseline forecasts, which use weighted averages and regression to the mean to estimate a player's current true talent level; and
3. Aging curves, which uses the career paths of comparable players to estimate how a player's statistics are likely to change over time.

With all those important things covered, let's take a look at what's in the book this year.

Team Prospectus

You bought this book to learn more about your favorite (or maybe least-favorite, who are we to judge?) team, so let's talk about them. After a thoughtful preview of the 2019 season, you'll be presented with our Team Prospectus. This outlines many of the key statistics for each team's 2018 season, as well as a very inviting stadium diagram.

First you'll find the Performance Graphs page. The first is the 2018 Hit List Ranking. This shows our Hit List Rank for the team on each day of the 2018 season and is intended to give you a picture of the ups and downs of the team's season, including their highest and lowest ranks of the year. Hit List Rank measures overall team performance and drives the Hit List Power Rankings at the baseballprospectus.com website.

The second graph is Committed Payroll and helps you see how the team's payroll has compared to the MLB and divisional average payrolls over time. Payroll figures are currents as of January 1, 2019; with so many free agents still unsigned as of this writing, the final 2018 figure will likely be significantly different for many teams. (In the meantime, you can always find the most current data at Baseball Prospectus' Cot's Baseball Contracts page.)

The third graph is Farm System Ranking and displays how the Baseball Prospectus prospect team has ranked the organization's farm system since 2007. It also indicates the highest and lowest ranks that the farm system achieved over that time.

We start the Team Performance page with the squad's unadjusted and third-order 2018 win-loss records, presented in divisional context. We then list the three highest performing hitters and pitchers by WARP for 2018. Beneath that are a host of other team statistics. **Pythag** presents an adjusted 2018 winning percentage, calculated by taking runs scored per game (**RS/G**) and runs allowed per game (**RA/G**) for the team, and running them through a version of Bill James' Pythagorean formula that was refined and improved by David Smyth and Brandon Heipp. (The formula is called "Pythagenpat," which is equally fun to type and to say.)

Next up is **DRC+**, described earlier, to indicate the overall hitting ability of the team either above or below league-average. Run prevention on the pitching side is covered by **DRA** (also mentioned earlier) and another metric: Fielding Independent Pitching (**FIP**), which calculates another ERA-like statistic based on strikeouts, walks, and home runs recorded. Defensive Efficiency Rating (**DER**) tells us the percentage of balls in play turned into outs for the team, and is a quick fielding shorthand that rounds out run prevention.

After that, we have several measures related to roster composition, as opposed to on-field performance. **B-Age** and **P-Age** tell us the average age of a team's batters and pitchers, respectively. **Salary** is the combined team payroll for all on-field players, and Doug Pappas' Marginal Dollars per Marginal Win (**M$/MW**) tells us how much money a team spent to earn production above replacement level.

Ending this batch of statistics is the number of disabled list days a team had over the season (**DL Days**) and the amount of salary paid to players on the disabled list (**$ on DL**); this final number is expressed as a percentage of total payroll.

Next to each of these stats, we've listed each team's MLB rank in that category from 1st to 30th. In this, 1st always indicates a positive outcome and 30th a negative outcome, except in the case of salary–1st is highest.

The Team Projections page is intended to convey the team's operational capacity entering the 2019 season. We start with the team's PECOTA projected record for 2019, again in divisional context. The **+/-** column indicates how many more or less wins the team is projected to get than they got in 2018. We then list the three highest projected hitters and pitchers by WARP for 2018. A brief farm system summary follows, with the team's top prospect and number of BP Top 101 Prospects. Finally, we list the key new players and departed players, along with their 2019 projected WARP.

Alex Bregman 3B

Born: 03/30/94 Age: 25 Bats: R Throws: R
Height: 6'0" Weight: 180 Origin: Round 1, 2015 Draft (#2 overall)

YEAR	TEAM	LVL	AGE	PA	R	2B	3B	HR	RBI	BB	K	SB	CS	AVG/OBP/SLG
2016	CCH	AA	22	285	54	16	2	14	46	42	26	5	3	.297/.415/.559
2016	FRE	AAA	22	83	17	6	0	6	15	5	12	2	1	.333/.373/.641
2016	HOU	MLB	22	217	31	13	3	8	34	15	52	2	0	.264/.313/.478
2017	HOU	MLB	23	626	88	39	5	19	71	55	97	17	5	.284/.352/.475
2018	HOU	MLB	24	705	105	51	1	31	103	96	85	10	4	.286/.394/.532
2019	HOU	MLB	25	675	96	38	3	23	78	73	107	12	4	.272/.359/.463

Breakout: 6%   Improve: 52%   Collapse: 5%   Attrition: 2%   MLB: 100%
Comparables: Anthony Rendon, David Wright, Pablo Sandoval

YEAR	TEAM	LVL	AGE	PA	DRC+	VORP	BABIP	BRR	FRAA	WARP
2016	CCH	AA	22	285	172	38.9	.286	1.6	SS(51): -3.4, 3B(11): 1.4	2.7
2016	FRE	AAA	22	83	161	10.0	.333	-1.2	SS(14): 2.1, LF(3): -0.1	0.8
2016	HOU	MLB	22	217	107	9.6	.317	0.5	3B(40): 0.9, SS(6): -0.1	1.1
2017	HOU	MLB	23	626	114	34.7	.311	-1.5	3B(132): 8.7, SS(30): -2.9	3.9
2018	HOU	MLB	24	705	150	72.6	.289	-1.6	3B(136): 5.4, SS(28): -0.4	7.4
2019	HOU	MLB	25	675	125	37.3	.295	0.0	3B 7, SS 0	4.6

After the projections page, we share a few items about the team's home ballpark. There's the aforementioned diagram of the park's dimensions (including distances to the outfield wall), a few important biographical facts about the stadium, a graphic showing the height of the wall from the left-field pole to the right-field pole, and a table showing three-year park factors for the stadium. The park factors are displayed as indexes where 100 is average, 110 means that the park inflates the statistic in question by 10 percent, and 90 means that the park deflates the statistic in question by 10 percent.

Following the ballpark page, we have a **Personnel** section that lists many of the important decision-makers and upper-level field and operations staff members for the franchise, as well as any former Baseball Prospectus staff members who are currently part of the organization.

Position Players

After all that information and a thoughtful bylined essay covering each team, we present our player comments. Each player is listed with the major-league team who employed him as of early January 2019. If a player changed teams after that point via free agency, trade, or any other method, you'll be able to find them in the book for their previous squad.

First, we cover biographical information (age is as of June 30, 2019) before moving onto the stats themselves. Our statistic columns include standard identifying information like **YEAR**, **TEAM**, **LVL** (level of affiliated play) and **AGE** before getting into the numbers. Next, we provide raw, unstranslated numbers like you might find on the back of your dad's baseball cards: **PA** (plate appearances), **R** (runs), **2B** (doubles), **3B** (triples), **HR** (home runs), **RBI** (runs batted in), **BB** (walks), **K** (strikeouts), **SB** (stolen bases) and **CS** (caught stealing). Then we have unadjusted "slash" statistics: **AVG** (batting average), **OBP** (on-base percentage) and **SLG** (slugging percentage).

Just below the stats box is **PECOTA** data, which is discussed further in a following section. After that, it's on to a pithy and always-informative comment written by a member of the Baseball Prospectus staff, before we cover more stats.

The second text box repeats YEAR, TEAM, LVL, AGE, and PA, then moves on to **DRC+** (Deserved Runs Created Plus), which we described earlier as total offensive expected contribution compared to the league average. Next, one of our oldest active metrics, **VORP** (Value Over Replacement Player), considers offensive production, position and plate appearances. In essence, it is the number of runs contributed beyond what a replacement-level player at the same position would contribute if given the same percentage of team plate appearances. VORP does not consider the quality of a player's defense.

BABIP (batting average on balls in play) tells us how often a ball in play fell for a hit, and can help us identify whether a batter may have been lucky or not ... but note that high BABIPs also tend to follow the great hitters of our time, as well as speedy singles hitters who put the ball on the ground.

The next item is **BRR** (Baserunning Runs), which covers all of a player's baserunning accomplishments which includes (but isn't limited to) swiped bags and failed attempts. Next is **FRAA** (Fielding Runs Above Average), which also includes the number of games previously played at each position noted in parentheses. Multi-position players have only their two most frequent positions listed here, but their total FRAA number reflects all positions played.

Our last column here is **WARP** (Wins Above Replacement Player). WARP estimates the total value of a player, which means for hitters it takes into account hitting runs above average (calculated using the DRC+ model), BRR and FRAA. Then, it makes an adjustment for positions played and gives the player a credit for plate appearances based upon the difference between "replacement level"¬–which is derived from the quality of players added to a team's roster after the start of the season¬–and the league average.

Catchers

Catchers are a special breed, and thus they have earned their own separate box which displays some of the defensive metrics that we've built just for them. As an example, let's check out J.T. Realmuto.

YEAR	TEAM	P. COUNT	FRM RUNS	BLK RUNS	THRW RUNS	TOT RUNS
2016	MIA	18935	-8.5	1.8	2.1	-5.6
2017	MIA	18959	5.3	1.7	1.0	9.1
2018	MIA	16399	-0.4	0.9	0.1	0.4
2019	PHI	18448	-1.4	1.5	0.7	0.8

The **YEAR** and **TEAM** columns match what you'd find in the other stat box. **P. COUNT** indicates the number of pitches thrown while the catcher was behind the plate, including swinging strikes, fouls, and balls in play. **FRM RUNS** is the total run value the catcher provided (or cost) his team by influencing the umpire to call strikes where other catchers did not. **BLK RUNS** expresses the total run value above or below average for the catcher's ability to prevent wild pitches and passed balls. **THRW RUNS** is calculated using a similar model as the previous two statistics, and it measures a catcher's ability to throw out basestealers but also to dissuade them from testing his arm in the first place. It takes into account factors like the pitcher (including his delivery and pickoff move) and baserunner (who could be as fast as Billy Hamilton or as slow as Yonder Alonso). **TOT RUNS** is the sum of all of the previous three statistics.

Pitchers

Let's give our pitchers a turn, using 2018 NL Cy Young winner Jacob deGrom as our example. Take a look at his first stat block: the first line and the **YEAR**, **TEAM**, **LVL** and **AGE** columns are the same as in the position player example earlier.

Here too, we have a series of columns that display raw, unadjusted statistics compiled by the pitcher over the course of a season: **W** (wins), **L** (losses), **SV** (saves), **G** (games pitched), **GS** (games started), **IP** (innings pitched), **H** (hits allowed) and **HR** (home runs allowed). Next we have two statistics that are rates: **BB/9** (walks per nine innings) and **K/9** (strikeouts per nine innings), before returning to the unadjusted **K** (strikeouts).

Next up is **GB%** (ground ball percentage), which is the percentage of all batted balls that were hit in the ground, including both outs and hits. Remember, this is based on observational data and subject to human error, so please approach this with a healthy dose of skepticism.

BABIP (batting average on balls in play) is calculated using the same methodology as it is for position players, but it often tells us more about a pitcher than it does a hitter. With pitchers, a high BABIP is often due to poor defense or bad luck, and can often be an indicator of potential rebound, and a low BABIP may be cause to expect performance regression. (A typical league-average BABIP is close to .290-.300.)

After a witty 150ish words on the player like only Baseball Prospectus's staff can provide, it's on to that second stat block, which repeats the YEAR, TEAM, LVL, and AGE columns. The metrics **WHIP** (walks plus hits per inning pitched) and **ERA**

Seattle Mariners 2019

(earned run average) are old standbys: WHIP measures walks and hits allowed on a per-inning basis, while ERA measures earned runs on a nine-inning basis. Neither of these stats are translated or adjusted.

DRA (Deserved Run Average) was described at length earlier, and measures how many runs the pitcher "deserved" to allow per nine innings. Please note that since we lack all the data points that would make for a "real" DRA for minor-league events, the DRA displayed for minor league partial-seasons is based off of different data. (That data is a modified version of our cFIP metric, which you can find more information about on our website.)

Jacob deGrom   RHP
Born: 06/19/88   Age: 31   Bats: L   Throws: R
Height: 6'4"   Weight: 180   Origin: Round 9, 2010 Draft (#272 overall)

YEAR	TEAM	LVL	AGE	W	L	SV	G	GS	IP	H	HR	BB/9	K/9	K	GB%	BABIP
2016	NYN	MLB	28	7	8	0	24	24	148	142	15	2.2	8.7	143	47%	.312
2017	NYN	MLB	29	15	10	0	31	31	201[1]	180	28	2.6	10.7	239	48%	.305
2018	NYN	MLB	30	10	9	0	32	32	217	152	10	1.9	11.2	269	48%	.281
2019	NYN	MLB	31	13	9	0	31	31	186	145	18	2.3	10.7	221	46%	.286

Breakout: 8%   Improve: 29%   Collapse: 28%   Attrition: 6%   MLB: 85%
Comparables: Erik Bedard, A.J. Burnett, CC Sabathia

YEAR	TEAM	LVL	AGE	WHIP	ERA	DRA	WARP	MPH	FB%	WHF	CSP
2016	NYN	MLB	28	1.20	3.04	3.30	3.5	96.3	59.6	12.1	47.2
2017	NYN	MLB	29	1.19	3.53	3.02	5.7	97.2	55.5	14.5	49.5
2018	NYN	MLB	30	0.91	1.70	2.09	8.0	98.2	52.1	16.3	48.4
2019	NYN	MLB	31	1.02	2.91	3.23	3.9	96.6	54.5	14.8	48.2

Just like with hitters, **WARP** (Wins Above Replacement Player) is a total value metric that puts pitchers of all stripes on the same scale as position players. We use DRA as the primary input for our calculation of WARP. You might notice that relief pitchers (due to their limited innings) may have a lower WARP than you were expecting or than you might see in other WARP-like metrics. WARP does not take leverage into account, just the actions a pitcher performs and the expected value of those actions ... which ends up judging high-leverage relief pitchers differently than you might imagine given their prestige and market value.

MPH gives you the pitcher's 95th percentile velocity for the noted season, in order to give you an idea of what the *peak* fastball velocity a pitcher possesses. Since this comes from our pitch tracking data, it is not publicly available for minor-league pitchers.

Finally, we display the three new pitching metrics we described earlier. **FB%** (fastball percentage) gives you the percentage of fastballs thrown out of all pitches. **WhiffRt** (whiff rate) tells you the percentage of swinging strikes induced out of all pitches. **CS Prob** (called strike probability) expresses the likelihood of all pitches thrown to result in a called strike, after controlling for factors like handedness, umpire, pitch type, count, and location.

PECOTA

All players have PECOTA projections for 2019, as well as a set of other numbers that describe the performance of comparable players according to PECOTA. All projections for 2019 are for the player at the date we went to press in early January and are projected into the league and park context as indicated by the team abbreviation. All PECOTA projected statistics represent a player's projected major-league performance.

The numbers beneath the player's stats—Breakout, Improve, Collapse, Attrition—are part and parcel of the PECOTA projections. They estimate the likelihood of changes in performance relative to the player's previously-established level of production, based on the performance of comparable players:

Breakout Rate is the percent change that a player's production will improve by at least 20 percent relative to the weighted average of his performance over his most recent seasons.

Improve Rate is the percent chance that a player's production will improve at all relative to his baseline performance. A player who is expected to perform just the same as he has in the recent past will have an Improve Rate of 50 percent.

Collapse Rate is the percent chance that a position player's production will decline by at least 25 percent relative to his baseline performance.

Attrition Rate operates on playing time rather than performance. Specifically, it measures the likelihood that a player's playing time will decrease by at least 50 percent relative to his established level.

Breakout Rate and Collapse Rate can sometimes be counterintuitive for players who have already experienced a radical change in performance level. It's also worth noting that the projected decline in a player's rate performances might not be indicative of an expected decline in underlying ability or skill, but could just be an anticipated correction following a breakout season.

MLB% is the percentage of similar players who played in the major leagues in their relevant season.

The final pieces of information are the player's three highest-scoring comparable players as determined by PECOTA. All comparables represent a snapshot of how the listed player was performing at the same age as the current player, so if a 23-year-old pitcher is compared to Bartolo Colon, he's actually being compared to a 23-year-old Colon, not the version that pitched for the Rangers in 2018, nor to Colon's career as a whole.

A few points about pitcher projections. First, we aren't yet projecting peak velocity, so that column will be blank in the PECOTA lines. Second, projecting DRA is trickier than evaluating past performance, because it is unclear how deserving each pitcher will be of his anticipated outcomes. However, we know that another DRA-related statistic–contextual FIP or cFIP–estimates future run scoring very well. So for PECOTA, the projected DRA figures you see are based on the past cFIPs generated by the pitcher and comparable players over time, along with the other factors described above.

Lineouts

In each chapter's Lineouts section, you'll find abbreviated text comments, as well as most of same information you'd find in our full player comments. We limit the stats boxes in this section to only including the 2018 information for each player.

Exclusive Player Visualizations

In our constant battle to provide you with new and interesting baseball content you can't find anywhere else, we've added a trio of data visualizations to each hitter's entry in these books and a pair of visualizations for each pitcher.

For hitters, you'll find three new infographics. The first is each player's **Batted Ball Distribution**, which displays the five major sections of the field: LF (left), LCF (left center), CF (center), RCF (right center), and RF (right). The percentage indicated tells us what percentage of batted balls from that hitter fell within that part of the field during the 2018 season. We've also included the hitter's slugging percentage on balls in play (also called **SLGCON**) for that part of the field.

You'll also see two heatmaps: **Strike Zone vs LHP** and **Strike Zone vs RHP**. These heat maps represent a view of the strike zone from behind the catcher. Areas where there is a darker coloration represent the places where a higher percentage of pitches resulted in hits. In other words, the heatmap represents a hitter's "sweet spots" for getting hits against either left-handed or right-handed pitchers, depending on the image.

Pitchers get two images that help explain what their pitches look like from a hitter's perspective: **Pitch Shape vs LHH** and **Pitch Shape vs RHH**. These images show you the shape and the "tunneling" effect of each pitcher's offerings from the batter's perspective. For each type of pitch that a pitcher throws (represented by an indicator shape), there's a set of dots indicating the flight path, where each dot represents a 0.01-second interval. This maps the average trajectory and speed of an offering, ending where the ball crosses the plate. The solid black box represents the regular strike zone, while the gray contour lines indicate the range of locations that a pitcher typically works in.

Below the image, we provide a bit more detailed information about each pitcher's average offering in the **Pitch Types** box. Here, we also list each of the pitcher's major offerings under the **Type** column.

- **Fastballs** (which usually refers to the four-seam variation)
- **Sinkers** and/or two-seam fastballs
- **Cutters** (which could include "hard" cutters like cut fastballs and "soft" cutters that resemble hard sliders)
- **Changeups** (not including most splitters)
- **Splitters** (split-fingered pitches, forkballs, and some split-changes)
- **Sliders** and/or slurves
- **Curveballs** (including spike-curveballs and knuckle-curveballs, as well as some slurvy curves)
- **Slow curveballs** and/or eephus pitches
- **Knuckleballs**
- **Screwballs**

The **Freq** column indicates the percentage of overall pitches that fall into each of those type categories; if a pitcher has a 16.55% score for changeups, then that's the percent of all pitches that he throws as changeups. **Velo** is exactly what you think it is: the average miles per hour for each pitch type. **H Mov** is the number of inches of horizontal movement on the average pitch of that type, while **V Mov** is the number of inches of vertical movement on the average pitch of that type. (At Baseball Prospectus, we measure this over the long flight of the ball and include gravity into the V Mov number in order to give you the most realistic representation of what the pitch *actually* does.)

If you're wondering about the second number in brackets, that's the index for that velocity or movement compared to the league average. Like DRC+, a score of 100 means that the speed or movement is about the same as league average, while a higher score means that there's higher velocity or movement than the league average. Numbers below 100 indicate less velocity or movement than the league average.

Part 1: Team Analysis

Table for Two: Previewing the 2019 Seattle Mariners

Nathan Bishop and Matt Ellis

NATHAN BISHOP: Matt, hi. I was trying to think of the best way to describe to people how long it's been since the Mariners have been to the playoffs and, while I'm sure this isn't it, it's important to understand that when it happened Sugar Ray, Staind, and Lifehouse were all a very big deal.

Matt, it's 2019, and PECOTA projects the Mariners for 72 wins, and a fourth-place finish in the AL West. What are we to make of all this?

MATT ELLIS: There is a commercial I used to hear on the radio all the time from a roofing company. I forget the name of the company, but it would start out with a narrator's banal, inoffensive voice reading off a list of historical events to the listener, but it soon became clear that something wasn't quite right, time was out of joint, that he was clearly describing some ancient historical period. Box office returns from *Spider-Man 2*, the Old Navy boot-cut jean craze. Something about the new blue brick Nokia cell phone you just bought. Then, suddenly, he would be like–*ah, gotcha! These events from a lifetime ago are as old as your ROOF! DO YOU REALLY TRUST SAM RAIMI'S SPIDER-MAN 2 TO PROTECT YOUR LIVING ROOM FROM LEAKS?* It was mostly to get you freaking out that you need to immediately re-shingle your roof, but all I could think about was that, *man*, I remember seeing *Spider-Man 2* in theaters, and sure, I had weird zits and wore boot-cut jeans, but it wasn't really *that* long ago.

You might think this is off topic, but we're here today talking about the Seattle Mariners and playoff baseball, as well as the team's current projection to win 72 games and finish fourth in the AL West. Oddly enough, both those concepts have a lot in common with boot-cut jeans, which are apparently making a comeback: the Mariners being both bad *and* good are both historical concepts as old as your old roof. You definitely should replace it, but it's just gonna leak again, sooner than you think.

NATHAN: Jack Zduriencik + wig = Doc Ock. I think we can all, in these divisive times, at least agree on that.

MATT: I know I do. Nathan, in recent years Mariners fans have been split between wings which seemed to have faith, on the one hand, that the 2018 roster as constructed had another run in them, and on the other, those who felt that regardless of how the Wild Card spots unfolded, the band-aid was going to have to come off sooner or later. We know which path they chose, as you note above: the latter. So what do you make of the team's approach the 2018-19 offseason, and did they do well given their aims?

NATHAN: So basically General Manager Jerry Dipoto ended 2018 by meeting with the media, put his hand on the (HOLY BOOK OF CHOICE GOES HERE), raised his hand and said "You all I am done with trades for a bit Imma chill I swear." Within a month of doing that he traded James Paxton to the Yankees, Robinson Cano and Edwin Diaz to the Mets, Mike Zunino to the Rays, and Jean Segura to the Phillies.

Following the team in the Dipoto Era has made answering the question complicated because, while he maintains a ceaseless level of activity, it's pretty hard to really tell what the end goal of all this is. After spending his first three years telling everyone the team wasn't going to rebuild, the team now is clearly doing that, even though he has branded it a "Step back". So, in that sense, I guess they've done fairly well?

The farm system, which spent the last three seasons as arguably the worst in the game, now people are saying "Wow the poisonous gas in here isn't nearly as choking as it once was." After acquiring Justus Sheffield, Erik Swanson, Jarred Kelenic, Jake Fraley, J.P. Crawford, Justin Dunn, and Shed Long among others, one could even be forgiven for calling the Mariners farm "ok". Is this the goal? Matt, I submit to you: I have no idea.

MATT: I think you're approaching the true essence of the issue with your response here. I suppose question that *really* matters for the 2019 Seattle Mariners is not "did they do well (in the offseason) given their aims?" but is "how will they be able to re-cast their aims *a posteriori* in order to prove they indeed did well, *as you can see by their aims?*" Or, perhaps a better way of saying it is that aims and results for Jerry Dipoto, in his brief tenure in Seattle, have proven to be pretty malleable. I don't quite blame the guy–who could, after inheriting the decade-long mess he did?–but at the same time, improving what was by all accounts the worst farm system *in the entire game of baseball* to a respectable B average should be reason to celebrate on its own!

And yet, there he was, declaring as if self-evident that the Mariners weekend-long turn around suddenly gave them one of the best farm systems in the entire league. I can't quite blame him: I wonder how much this kind of hyperbolizing is related to job security, or what have you. But with a fanbase that has spent almost *two decades* oscillating between accidental success (which always, inevitably failed) and having your heart torn out of your ribcage and set on fire like in *The Temple of Doom*, well then good lord, man! A respectable plan is all you need!

You know, that makes this all the more frustrating: the Mariners *absolutely* did well in the offseason, given their aims. But it's troubling that just well doesn't seem to be good enough, discursively, for this front office. Which makes me terrified for what will happen when they get their first season-ending knee injury, their first clubhouse fight, their first coach resignation. So Nathan, enough talk of the eternal return, as much as we all know it's coming. Who are you looking forward to watching in 2019, which player should Mariners fans hitch their hopes onto in the wake of such expansive roster turnover?

NATHAN: You know before I answer that let me just say that I think the greater baseball universe needs to appreciate how much our experience as Mariner fans has conditioned me to think that by answering that question honestly I am positioning baby grand connected to rapidly fraying wire directly over the head of whichever player I mention. Everyone uses the Mets as the punchline for baseball's own riff on "THE ARISTOCRATS" but they have two championships, and played in a World Series less than five years ago. Mariner fans would commit deeply heinous acts to inherit that kind of curse.

Ok, sorry, I had to get that out. Now at great risk to my emotional health and undoubtedly his future prospects the answer is LHP Yusei Kikuchi. Easily the biggest free agent acquisition of the Dipoto Era, the 27-year old starter brings strong pedigree from the NPL, and has shown a promising mix of stuff and deceptive delivery. One scout I spoke to raved that Kikuchi's athleticism, deception, and delivery repeatability were "among the best he had ever seen" so yeah, engage the Hype Train. Next stop, DOOMSVILLE.

Matt, here is my question to you. Assuming the Great One is not freed from his watery prison to rise and devour the universe in fire and ash, how do you think Mariner fans will look back at the 2019 in, say, five years from now?

MATT: Well, hopefully it will be the exciting version of the answer you just gave: the year perennial All-Star and Mariners franchise icon Yusei Kikuchi tore the AL West a new one, setting up the M's to finally break free from their quarter-century slumber. But truth be told, it would be remarkably unfair to put that kind of franchise pressure on the guy (I mean, what's stopped them from doing that to anyone before?). My hope, as a fan, is that some new faces show promise and that I actually want to hop on Twitter the day after a game I missed to see if so-and-so did something Cool and Neat. I think that's a good goal for 2024's 2019 retrospective.

NATHAN: Does this mean we have to have Twitter still in 2024?

MATT: Geez, man, I know we're a dark lot, but that's taking it *way too far*.

NATHAN: Matt, old sport, you're right and I apologize. Let's look towards something more "in the now" as they used (?) to say. Let's talk about Felix Hernandez, and his presumptive final season in Seattle. It is not going to be good, but I'm not sure that matters, either for the 2019 Mariners or his legacy. Do you disagree?

MATT: It will not be good, either way. I'm trying to decide what the best possible outcome might look like. Obviously, he isn't the pitcher he once was, but unlike other recent late-turnaround cases, he doesn't seem to have fully committed to a turnaround that realistically addresses what his physical limitations (and continued strengths!) are. I have a running conspiracy theory that this is in part because he already made a career-altering transition to deal with declining velocity, and it (plus his early success), has him thinking–*believing*–that all he has to do is find that little spot where it's always been, and just give it one more go. As a fan I'm gutted that one of the franchise's most iconic players could be ending his time here in this manner, but like you said, I kind of wonder if the coda has already been played, the final refrain having been repeated before jumping ahead to the end.

To ventriloquize Jerry Dipoto, then, in the spirit of your previous question: how will this team end up by the end of the season (and how will it be Felix's fault), and what kind of path will they take to get there?

NATHAN: Well it will be Felix's fault because the Mariners traded away one of baseball's better defensive catchers in Mike Zunino, replaced him with maybe its worst in Omar Narvaez, and could desperately use a starting pitcher with above average stuff that has thrown more than zero regular season innings on the continent of the Americas.

In reality, though, I think this team may just jump out to an enjoyable start. Clearly the pitching could completely nuke them, and while improved, the organizational depth still makes any significant injury a potential disaster. However, for a team that's lost Jean Segura, Robinson Cano, Nelson Cruz, and Zunino the lineup should, at least before Jerry trades anything costing more than a wooden nickel, be fun to watch. The addition of Edwin Encarnacion and Domingo Santana should offset a good portion of the lost power from last year, and with Mitch Haniger looking like a star, and Narvaez's bat intriguing, Seattle is only a realistic bounceback season from Dee Gordon and/or Kyle Seager from scaring plenty of pitchers this year.

So, I say they plug away the first few months at or around .500. Maybe they catch a hot streak that has them in the "if the season ended today" Wild Card conversation through June. Eventually, attrition will have its due, and the team will fade. The season will shift away from the joy of the occasional Jay Bruce shot off the Hit It Here Cafe and whatever handshakes Gordon and Tim Beckham come up with to the true focus of the organization: Which parts of this team's newly-competent farm system look like they can develop into the foundation of the next (not only, you jokers. 2001 exists) great Mariners roster.

That said I do like the upside in Kikuchi, and see more coming from Gordon and Seager than PECOTA so I'll take the over on 72 wins. I'm calling this a 78-win 2019, and third place. How do you see it?

MATT: The pessimist in me notes that your 2019 upside–dancing around .500 and contending with the Wild Card before fading–was quite literally the best possible outcome of the past six or so years. I didn't hate it all, so I suppose, sign me up! I'm feeling somewhere in the mid-70s as well. But the real test, I think, will be in hoping nobody (and I mean *nobody*) starts taking win percentage seriously by May. If we take Dipoto at his word, the plan is for the team to build itself in order to compete by 2021, or 2020 at the *absolute earliest*. I suppose they could surprise everyone with an exciting 2019 season, but the risks that come with pushing it, in my opinion, far outweigh the responsibility to set this roster up for continued future success, which is supposedly the plan (i.e., Royals GM Dayton Moore is *not* on the event invite).

NATHAN: So, what we're saying is for the Seattle Mariners, arguably baseball's saddest franchise, to finally be good, we must pray to all we hold dear they are kind of bad this year?

MATT: #TrueToTheBlue

Performance Graphs

2018 Hit List Ranking

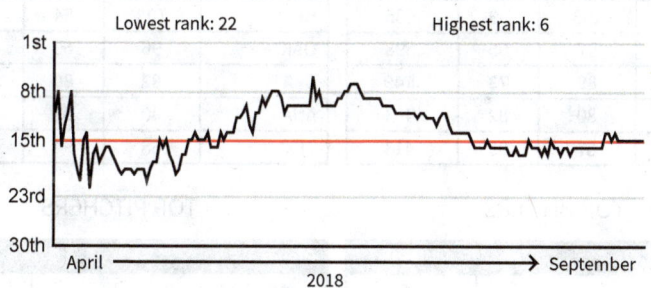

Committed Payroll (in millions)

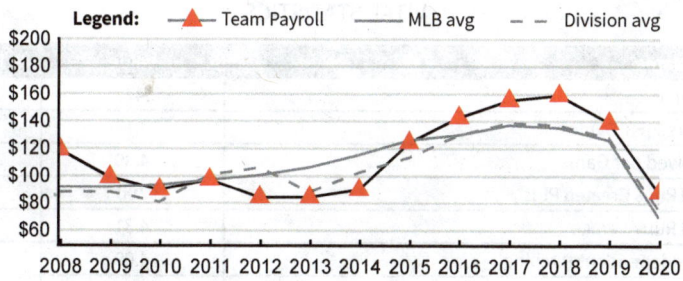

Farm System Ranking

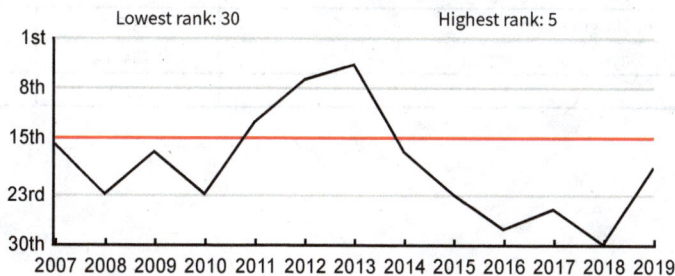

2018 Team Performance

ACTUAL STANDINGS

Team	W	L	Pct
HOU	103	59	.635
OAK	97	65	.598
SEA	**89**	**73**	**.549**
ANA	80	82	.493
TEX	67	95	.413

THIRD-ORDER STANDINGS

Team	W	L	Pct
HOU	108	54	.666
OAK	96	66	.592
SEA	**82**	**80**	**.506**
ANA	80	82	.493
TEX	68	94	.419

TOP HITTERS

Player	WARP
Mitch Haniger	3.9
Jean Segura	3.5
Nelson Cruz	3.1

TOP PITCHERS

Player	WARP
James Paxton	4.9
Marco Gonzales	3.3
Edwin Diaz	2.7

VITAL STATISTICS

Statistic Name	Value	Rank
Pythagenpat	.477	18th
Runs Scored per Game	4.18	21st
Runs Allowed per Game	4.39	17th
Deserved Runs Created Plus	100	9th
Deserved Run Average	4.31	14th
Fielding Independent Pitching	4.09	17th
Defensive Efficiency Rating	.705	17th
Batter Age	29.8	29th
Pitcher Age	29.3	25th
Salary	$157.9M	11th
Marginal $ per Marginal Win	$3.6M	19th
Disabled List Days	$764.0M	3rd
$ on DL	20%	24th

2019 Team Projections

PROJECTED STANDINGS

Team	W	L	Pct	+/-
HOU	98	64	.604	-5
ANA	80	82	.493	0
OAK	79	83	.487	-18
TEX	71	91	.438	+4
SEA	**70**	**92**	**.432**	**-19**

TOP PROJECTED HITTERS

Player	WARP
Mitch Haniger	3.6
Edwin Encarnacion	2.9
Kyle Seager	2.0

TOP PROJECTED PITCHERS

Player	WARP
Marco Gonzales	1.7
Yusei Kikuchi	1.6
Mike Leake	1.2

FARM SYSTEM REPORT

Top Prospect	Number of Top 101 Prospects
Justus Sheffield, #50	2

KEY DEDUCTIONS

Player	WARP
James Paxton	3.8
Nelson Cruz	3.3
Robinson Cano	2.8
Jean Segura	2.6
Mike Zunino	2.1
Edwin Diaz	1.6
Alex Colome	0.6
Cameron Maybin	0.5
Ben Gamel	0.4
Juan Nicasio	0.3

KEY ADDITIONS

Player	WARP
Edwin Encarnacion	2.9
Jay Bruce	1.4
Mallex Smith	1.0
Domingo Santana	0.8
Justus Sheffield	0.7
Anthony Swarzak	0.3

Team Personnel

EVP, General Manager
Jerry Dipoto

VP, Assistant General Manager
Justin Hollander

VP, Scouting
Tom Allison

Special Assistant to General Manager
Joe Bohringer

Manager
Scott Servais

BP Alumni
John Choiniere
Jason Karegeannes

T-Mobile Park Stats

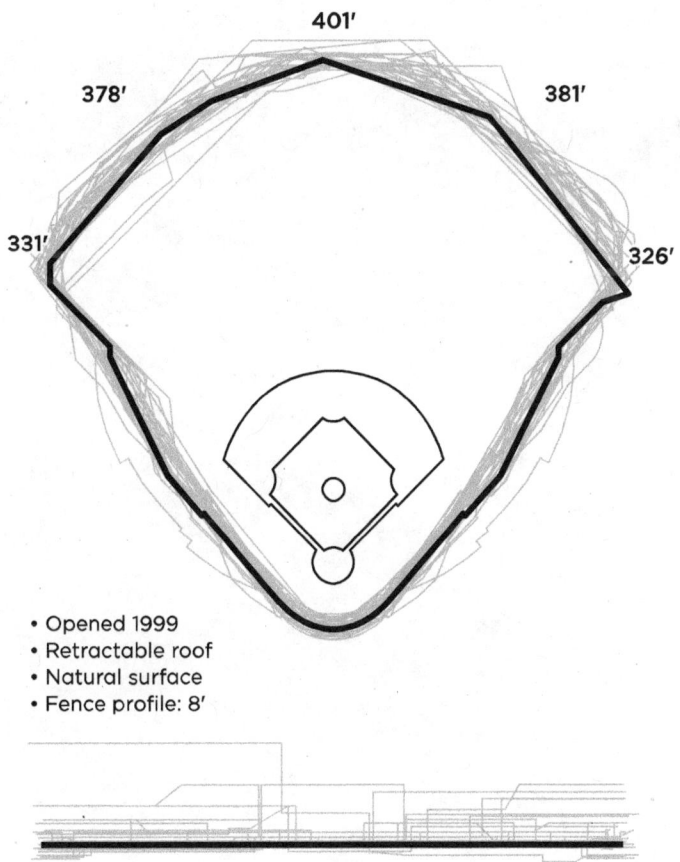

- Opened 1999
- Retractable roof
- Natural surface
- Fence profile: 8'

Three-Year Park Factors

Runs	Runs/RH	Runs/LH	HR/RH	HR/LH
96	96	94	102	100

Mariners Team Analysis

It is Tuesday, May 6th, 2008. Miguel Batista cuts through the fifty-two-degree air as he earns the Mariners' first out of the game, which just so happens to score Ian Kinsler from third base. It isn't quite *foggy*, but there is certainly something heavy sitting in the air. Maybe it's the brisk Pacific Northwest twilight, illuminated by the pale yellow of the LED scoreboard, causing Safeco Field to look like a helipad awaiting yet another nightly delivery of failure. Perhaps it was the carbon dioxide indifference of the 15,000 gathered in the stands on a Tuesday night; always a *Tuesday*, it seems. Nevertheless, it is one of *those* games which would come to define, if not just an era, perhaps the essence of Seattle's long-tortured ballclub. An operating theater of errors, surrounded by folded green plastic seats. A cool breeze.

Mariners fans are a wealthy bunch, in that they have such bountiful options to choose from in finding that one game to sum up what it has all been like. The elders point to the first decade of the franchise, which featured all from the above paragraph save for the frigid air and the live grass. That team found themselves aiming for the ceiling of a fourth-place finish under a concrete sky, but more often than not slipping to sixth, or seventh, the September conversation centering on just how soon the manager will be fired. *Wednesday, June 12th, 1985: White Sox 6, Mariners 3. 9,808 in attendance.* Switch the year out for one that begins with the number 2, and you wouldn't even think twice.

The anomaly, of course, are the Griffey nineties, the Ichiro early 2000s. '95 has become a groan-inducing signifier amidst the faithful, that year which saw the Mariners rally over a thirteen-game deficit to earn their first playoff berth. Both the elders and new blood would be quick to point out the irony that the most hapless team in Major League Baseball is *also* the team which tied the all-time single-season win total in 2001 with 116. Three years later it would be back to the Tuesdays and the 9,808s. The years since have brought with them endless cycles of tinkering, retooling, re-envisioning, re-marketing, each iteration promising that the lessons of the past had finally been learned: GM Bill Bavasi was fired in 2008 after he literally locked the team in the closet for a stern talking to, and ownership caught up with the times in appointing Brewers' Special Assistant to the GM Jack Zduriencik to the position. But promises of a cutting-edge scout/stat combo soon gave way to arguments over fonts in backroom powerpoint presentations, and so he had to go, too.

Seattle Mariners 2019

Jerry Dipoto arrived in Seattle in the final days of a losing 2015 season, inheriting eight years of Robinson Cano, an aging once-ace Felix Hernandez, a seemingly ageless Nelson Cruz, and a coterie of young-ish homegrown players who managed to stand out amidst seven years of drafting and busting: Kyle Seager, Mike Zunino, James Paxton, Taijuan Walker, Brad Miller, Chris Taylor, and so on. Despite the family tradition of failure, it wasn't the worst situation a new GM could be adopted into. A relatively stable core which only missed the playoffs by a game in 2014, and an opportunity to clean house and implement a vertically-integrated culture in the farm system.

But it soon became clear that Dipoto wasn't planning on implementing only a few small tweaks. He let go baseball's greatest tantrum auteur since Lou Piniella, manager Lloyd McClendon, replacing him with Jerry Lundegaard impersonator Scott Servais. He hired a sports psychologist to run the entire farm system, and invented a new job for a PhD Exercise Physiologist, Dr. Lorena Martin, who was set to be the first-ever Director of High Performance. This was a club that was going to have #synergy, run top to bottom with a Silicon Valley ethos of #disruption set to finally get the Mariners over that hurdle so frustratingly out of reach for so long.

Soon, everyone but the established core was shipped out in an attempt to re-imagine the roster Dipoto had inherited from Zduriencik in a new image. Some moves worked out quite well: Taijuan Walker and Ketel Marte were sent to the Diamondbacks to acquire Jean Segura and Mitch Haniger, both of whom would soon be representing Seattle in the All Star Game. He bought low on a few bounce-back candidates, and designed what was supposed to be one of the best defensive outfields in the club's history to mitigate a fly-ball pitching staff. But the tinkering and the tossing in left the Mariners with the worst farm system in the game. Yet still, on he went, *Trader Jerry*, gutting the system for marginal upgrades with an apparent goal of sneaking into the second Wild Card. Each autumn, the team's momentum appeared spent, and each winter, the team refused to go gentle.

Then, 2018: the Mariners came out of the gates with their best start in over a decade, at one point owning an 88.3 percent chance to make the playoffs. Vindication was in the air, vindication on behalf of a front office whose main goal always seemed to be less winning than *inventing new ways to win*. Dee Gordon, recently acquired from Miami, was sent out to roam centerfield because he was fast, and had a Gold Glove. Wade LeBlanc, who had nearly pitched himself out of a career, earned a multi-year extension after being picked up on a minor league contract. Edwin Diaz, a starter throughout his career in the minor leagues, torched the league as the club's first-ever 57-save closer.

Servais and Dipoto were extended mid-season. It was finally going to happen. But the Mariners were radically overplaying their Pythagorean record, and it caught up to them. First, it was Cano, suspended for 80 games in May after testing positive for a PED masking agent. Then, a fight in the clubhouse that spilled out right in front of the awaiting press. Tensions were mounting. Servais left Hernandez out to die for six innings in a brutal loss to the Rangers, then moved him to the bullpen to send a message. The trade deadline offered few reinforcements, as Dipoto had already given away just about everything he had short of starting a rebuild. In the final series of the season, Segura was benched for lack of hustle. You could read it in their faces, all of them, that they just wanted this whole thing to be over. And as soon as it was, Dr. Martin publicly accused the front office of racism and sexism after her contract wasn't renewed, culminating in a lawsuit and evoking a PR nightmare as the club began planning what to do for 2019. They still had no real prospects.

Amidst all this, or perhaps as a result, Jerry decided the only thing left to do was to tear it down to the foundation, put up a few earthquake-proof walls, and hope the new house stands stronger than the last. It remains to be seen just which warm bodies they will find to fill the double-digits required to field a team by the official rulebook over the next couple of years, but of course, the goal isn't next year. In essence, Dipoto's five-year plan is both a Nietzschean eternal return and a rebirth, an acknowledgement that the driver had the map upside-down. It is a realization that taking the right exit would require backtracking a few miles on the other side of the concrete divider, showing all those same road signs previously seen on the drive up. After stripping the roster down to its bare bones—sending their ace James Paxton to the Yankees, Cano and Diaz to the Mets, amongst others—the Mariners will once again be playing baseball on *Tuesday*. They will be lucky to win 80 games. None of that is new. But at the same time, it *will* be new: There are prospects again, for the first time since 2013, with new names, and new hopes. The system is far from elite, and they will have to strike gold in just about every last one of them for this to work. But it's a system, nonetheless.

By saying they aim to compete by 2021, Dipoto has given the Mariners an aggressive timeline which theoretically will allow them to compete with declining Astros, Yankees, and Red Sox cores. He has overturned his roster for a farm system in the matter of weeks, giving himself that opportunity at full synergy he dreamt of while playing out the hand of Jack Zduriencik. This will be the real test of his front office: not whether they can innovate or sell technocratic expertise, but to see if they can build a winning baseball team from the ground up. They certainly think they can do it.

For fans, however, the hope is unearned, as many Mariners faithful have begun to question just how many This Times they have the patience to sit through. They have sat through many a Tuesday, and you can't quite blame them for wanting something different for once, even if they know deep down inside the Astros are unbeatable, that Felix doesn't have it anymore, that *nobody* is coming through the pipeline for reinforcements. And even with a new set of prospects ready to blossom in the minor leagues, the past decade of Mariner player development hasn't exactly earned the benefit of the doubt by fans skeptical or not—see: Dustin Ackley, Justin Smoak, or Jesus Montero. Why trust them now? Fans want results, not more press conferences.

So the Mariners will play, they will play baseball on Tuesday, June 18th, 2019, and there will be 9,808 fans in attendance. This time, however, they will do it without a concrete dome, they will do it without an exciting young fireballer from Venezuela, the only thing worth watching while the rest of the club withers into oblivion. They will play in 2020 and they will play in 2021, and a young outfielder named Jarred Kelenic might make his major league debut as a pinch-hitter in the bottom of the eighth in a 6-0 loss to the Padres. He might stare at a few balls in the dirt and then make weak contact, dribbling the ball up the middle as he beats out the throw with his freshman legs. Fans might see this and think that thought that they had so many times before, *I was there for his first at-bat*, or *when will the store have his shirsey in*. They might see a 24-year old pitcher who did not spend the 2019 season on the Mariners notch eleven strikeouts in a meaningless start, and they might feel like their good faith has been rewarded, because they were there that day, that Tuesday, September 14th, 2021.

The Mariners will play, because the end of Tuesday brings yet another day. ■

—Matt Ellis is an author of Baseball Prospectus.

Part 2: Player Analysis

Tim Beckham INF

Born: 01/27/90 Age: 29 Bats: R Throws: R
Height: 6'1" Weight: 205 Origin: Round 1, 2008 Draft (#1 overall)

YEAR	TEAM	LVL	AGE	PA	R	2B	3B	HR	RBI	BB	K	SB	CS	AVG/OBP/SLG
2016	TBA	MLB	26	215	25	12	5	5	16	14	67	2	1	.247/.300/.434
2017	TBA	MLB	27	345	31	5	3	12	36	24	110	5	4	.259/.314/.407
2017	BAL	MLB	27	230	36	13	2	10	26	12	57	1	1	.306/.348/.523
2018	BAL	MLB	28	402	45	17	0	12	35	27	100	1	2	.230/.287/.374
2019	SEA	MLB	29	128	14	5	1	4	14	10	34	1	1	.241/.305/.405

Breakout: 5% Improve: 43% Collapse: 11% Attrition: 13% MLB: 99%
Comparables: Ian Desmond, Luis Aguayo, Khalil Greene

After the historically garbagetastic season the Orioles just had, it's hard to remember that in 2017, the team stood just one game out of a Wild Card spot as late as September 5. That late-season surge was spurred in part by trade deadline acquisition Beckham, whom the Rays flipped to their division rival in exchange for a short-season pitcher. He went on a tear that August, out-slugging Mike Trout for the month and making Tampa Bay look silly for essentially giving away a former #1 overall pick. However, Beckham came back to Earth in 2018; he suffered a groin strain in late April that kept him out until the end of June and never really got on track in the back half of the season. There are causes for optimism: his atrocious contact skills are growing less atrocious, and the quality of his contact doesn't explain the near-hundred-point drop in BABIP. Beckham, who made no secret of his desire to be an everyday shortstop while with Tampa Bay, will finally have a full season to do that in 2019, and perhaps shed the Buster Posey comparisons once and for all.

YEAR	TEAM	LVL	AGE	PA	DRC+	VORP	BABIP	BRR	FRAA	WARP
2016	TBA	MLB	26	215	78	5.2	.349	-0.9	SS(25): 1.5, 2B(19): -0.2	0.1
2017	TBA	MLB	27	345	97	11.0	.357	-0.4	SS(70): -2.2, 2B(17): -0.8	1.0
2017	BAL	MLB	27	230	98	18.2	.376	0.9	SS(49): 3.2	1.4
2018	BAL	MLB	28	402	82	5.1	.282	0.8	SS(49): -3.7, 3B(40): -2.2	0.2
2019	SEA	MLB	29	128	94	3.3	.303	-0.2	SS 0, 3B -1	0.2

Tim Beckham, continued

Batted Ball Distribution

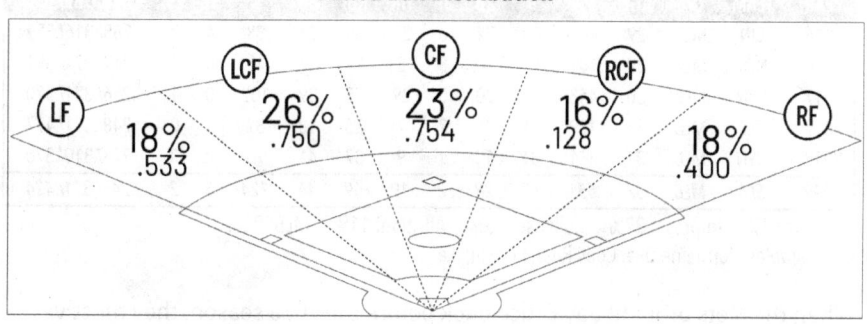

Strike Zone vs LHP

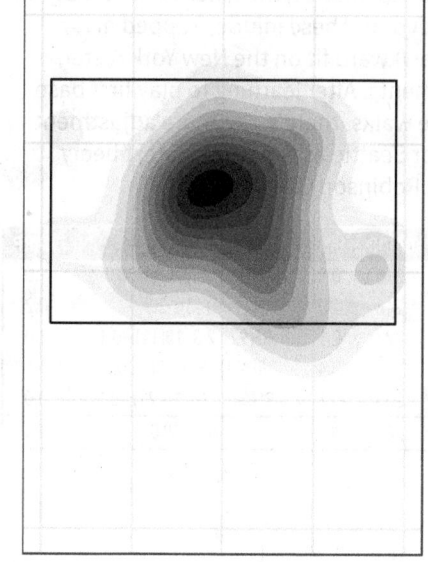

Strike Zone vs RHP

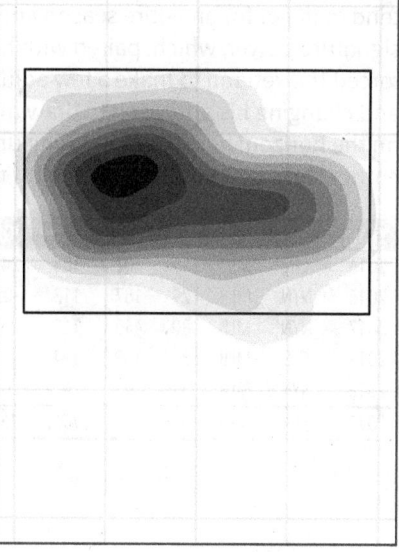

Seattle Mariners 2019

Jay Bruce RF
Born: 04/03/87   Age: 32   Bats: L   Throws: L
Height: 6'3"   Weight: 225   Origin: Round 1, 2005 Draft (#12 overall)

YEAR	TEAM	LVL	AGE	PA	R	2B	3B	HR	RBI	BB	K	SB	CS	AVG/OBP/SLG
2016	CIN	MLB	29	402	60	22	6	25	80	27	83	4	2	.265/.316/.559
2016	NYN	MLB	29	187	14	5	0	8	19	17	43	0	0	.219/.294/.391
2017	NYN	MLB	30	448	61	20	0	29	75	39	102	0	1	.256/.321/.520
2017	CLE	MLB	30	169	21	9	2	7	26	18	37	1	0	.248/.331/.477
2018	NYN	MLB	31	361	31	18	1	9	37	41	75	2	3	.223/.310/.370
2019	SEA	MLB	32	551	62	28	2	19	69	46	124	3	2	.245/.311/.424

Breakout: 4%   Improve: 37%   Collapse: 20%   Attrition: 11%   MLB: 92%
Comparables: Jermaine Dye, Cody Ross, Eric Hinske

When the Mets brought Jay Bruce back before the 2018 season, they must've expected him to be the same steadfast slugger he'd almost always been, good for 30 homers and a mildly disappointing on-base percentage. But last year was a disappointment for all parties, as Bruce spent extended time on the DL while dealing with nagging plantar fasciitis and hip injuries, the kinds of maladies that tend to linger for an entire season and beyond. These injuries sapped his signature power, which, paired with his awkward fit on the New York roster, forced the veteran to make a few adjustments. After learning to play first base and changing his approach to draw more walks, there's one more adjustment on the horizon: he'll now be suiting up for Seattle as the team's latest beefy corner slugger, a human reminder of the Robinson Cano era.

YEAR	TEAM	LVL	AGE	PA	DRC+	VORP	BABIP	BRR	FRAA	WARP
2016	CIN	MLB	29	402	108	24.4	.275	0.5	RF(95): -2.8, CF(1): 0.0	1.0
2016	NYN	MLB	29	187	113	-0.5	.246	-2.1	RF(43): -2.3	0.2
2017	NYN	MLB	30	448	115	25.6	.271	0.1	RF(92): 2.3, 1B(11): -0.1	2.0
2017	CLE	MLB	30	169	114	6.6	.283	0.4	RF(41): -2.7, 1B(1): 0.0	0.4
2018	NYN	MLB	31	361	91	1.9	.263	-1.8	RF(64): -0.6, 1B(21): -0.2	0.0
2019	SEA	MLB	32	551	100	13.8	.287	-1.1	LF 0, 1B 0	1.4

Jay Bruce, continued

Batted Ball Distribution

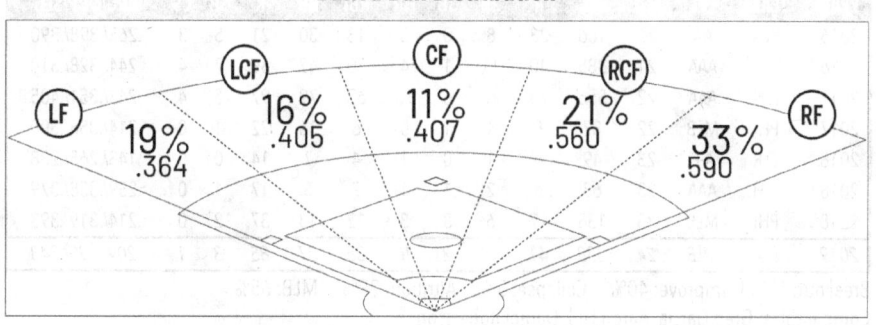

Strike Zone vs LHP

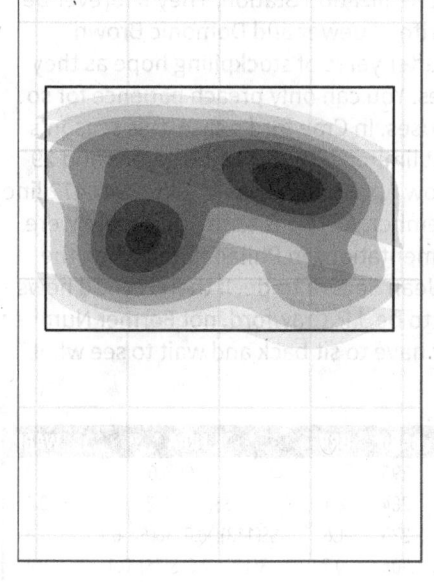

Strike Zone vs RHP

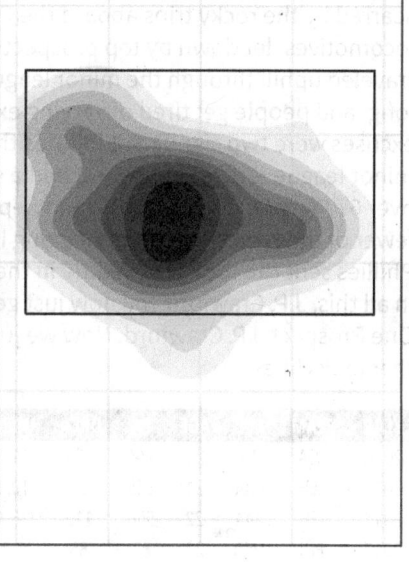

Seattle Mariners 2019

J.P. Crawford SS
Born: 01/11/95   Age: 24   Bats: L   Throws: R
Height: 6'2"   Weight: 180   Origin: Round 1, 2013 Draft (#16 overall)

YEAR	TEAM	LVL	AGE	PA	R	2B	3B	HR	RBI	BB	K	SB	CS	AVG/OBP/SLG
2016	REA	AA	21	166	23	8	0	3	13	30	21	5	3	.265/.398/.390
2016	LEH	AAA	21	385	40	11	1	4	30	42	59	7	4	.244/.328/.318
2017	LEH	AAA	22	556	75	20	6	15	63	79	97	5	4	.243/.351/.405
2017	PHI	MLB	22	87	8	4	1	0	6	16	22	1	0	.214/.356/.300
2018	CLR	A+	23	49	8	1	0	1	4	7	14	0	0	.143/.265/.238
2018	LEH	AAA	23	68	6	2	1	1	7	5	17	1	0	.259/.358/.379
2018	PHI	MLB	23	138	17	6	3	3	12	13	37	2	0	.214/.319/.393
2019	SEA	MLB	24	388	41	12	2	10	38	37	85	3	1	.209/.290/.343

Breakout: 12%   Improve: 40%   Collapse: 5%   Attrition: 29%   MLB: 65%
Comparables: Greg Garcia, Aaron Hill, Daniel Robertson

After a couple of years of riding a player's hype train once it gets rolling, Philadelphia fans get restless and antsy as passengers, wondering how much longer it'll be before they finally arrive at Realization Station. They'll forever be scarred by the rocky trips aboard the Carlton Loewer and Domonic Brown locomotives, let down by top prospects after years of stockpiling hope as they traveled uphill through the minor leagues. You can only preach patience for so long, and people get tired of varying excuses. In Crawford's case, this season's excuses were two significant injuries that limited him to 49 MLB games and 29 minor league and rehab games, and a slow April that masks a .245/.394/.472 line over 67 PA spread across June and September. All this is to say that there were fewer of the typical prospect-hugging lamentations in Philadelphia when the Phillies sent the rookie to Seattle in the Jean Segura trade. If there's good news in all this, J.P. Crawford will now just get to be J.P. Crawford, not Former Number One Prospect J.P. Crawford. Now we just have to sit back and wait to see what that looks like.

YEAR	TEAM	LVL	AGE	PA	DRC+	VORP	BABIP	BRR	FRAA	WARP
2016	REA	AA	21	166	139	11.7	.295	1.3	SS(36): 6.0	1.9
2016	LEH	AAA	21	385	89	10.4	.284	2.1	SS(87): -3.2	0.6
2017	LEH	AAA	22	556	113	28.4	.275	1.6	SS(113): -6.0, 3B(6): -0.7	1.8
2017	PHI	MLB	22	87	85	3.2	.306	-0.2	3B(13): 2.3, SS(6): 0.4	0.4
2018	CLR	A+	23	49	52	-1.5	.185	0.0	SS(8): -0.6, 3B(3): 0.5	-0.2
2018	LEH	AAA	23	68	84	2.8	.350	-1.7	SS(16): 0.2	-0.1
2018	PHI	MLB	23	138	78	4.7	.286	0.2	SS(30): 0.6, 3B(13): -0.6	0.2
2019	SEA	MLB	24	388	73	2.8	.245	0.0	SS 0	0.2

J.P. Crawford, continued

Batted Ball Distribution

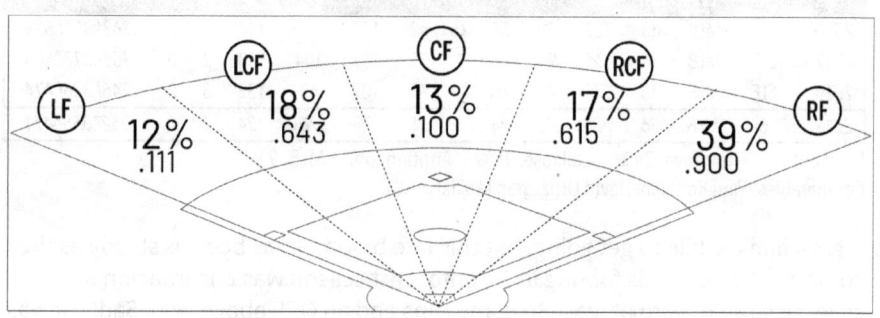

Strike Zone vs LHP **Strike Zone vs RHP**

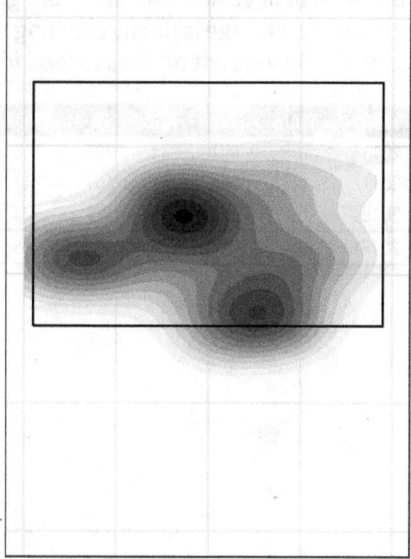

Seattle Mariners 2019

Edwin Encarnacion   DH
Born: 01/07/83   Age: 36   Bats: R   Throws: R
Height: 6'1"   Weight: 230   Origin: Round 9, 2000 Draft (#274 overall)

YEAR	TEAM	LVL	AGE	PA	R	2B	3B	HR	RBI	BB	K	SB	CS	AVG/OBP/SLG
2016	TOR	MLB	33	702	99	34	0	42	127	87	138	2	0	.263/.357/.529
2017	CLE	MLB	34	669	96	20	1	38	107	104	133	2	0	.258/.377/.504
2018	CLE	MLB	35	579	74	16	1	32	107	63	132	3	0	.246/.336/.474
2019	SEA	MLB	36	588	80	24	1	28	86	76	124	2	0	.252/.355/.471

Breakout: 1%   Improve: 24%   Collapse: 19%   Attrition: 6%   MLB: 91%
Comparables: Paul Konerko, David Ortiz, Stan Musial

It took him a while to get going, but this late bloomer has been as steady as they come since finding his footing in Toronto. Last season was Encarnacion's seventh straight with at least 30 home runs and an OPS above .800. Sadly, it was also a decline year. His ISO dropped for the fourth year in a row, he posted his highest strikeout rate since his rookie year and his walk rate sagged. It's hard to find hitters with Encarnacion's power who whiff as rarely as he does, so there's reason to believe he could age more gracefully than most 1B/DH masher types, but it looks like age is finally catching up to him. That said, the parrot should still have a good amount of rides to look forward to in 2019.

YEAR	TEAM	LVL	AGE	PA	DRC+	VORP	BABIP	BRR	FRAA	WARP
2016	TOR	MLB	33	702	138	28.7	.270	-0.4	1B(75): -2.8	3.9
2017	CLE	MLB	34	669	142	27.5	.271	-5.2	1B(23): -0.6	3.8
2018	CLE	MLB	35	579	125	12.9	.265	-5.1	1B(23): 0.8	2.1
2019	SEA	MLB	36	588	126	26.1	.280	-0.8	1B -1	2.9

Edwin Encarnacion, continued

Batted Ball Distribution

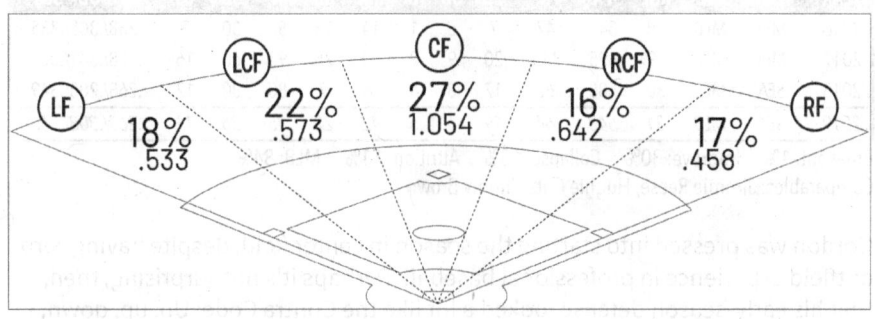

Strike Zone vs LHP   **Strike Zone vs RHP**

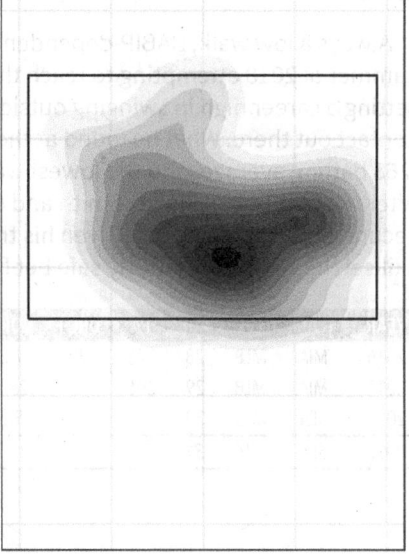

Dee Gordon 2B

Born: 04/22/88 Age: 31 Bats: L Throws: R
Height: 5'11" Weight: 170 Origin: Round 4, 2008 Draft (#127 overall)

YEAR	TEAM	LVL	AGE	PA	R	2B	3B	HR	RBI	BB	K	SB	CS	AVG/OBP/SLG
2016	MIA	MLB	28	345	47	7	6	1	14	18	55	30	7	.268/.305/.335
2017	MIA	MLB	29	695	114	20	9	2	33	25	93	60	16	.308/.341/.375
2018	SEA	MLB	30	588	62	17	8	4	36	9	80	30	12	.268/.288/.349
2019	SEA	MLB	31	543	64	19	6	5	42	22	85	36	11	.269/.308/.360

Breakout: 1% Improve: 30% Collapse: 13% Attrition: 11% MLB: 84%
Comparables: Jimmie Reese, Hughie Critz, Jimmy Brown

Gordon was pressed into starting the season in center field, despite having zero outfield experience in professional baseball. Perhaps it's not surprising, then, that his early-season defense looked a lot like the Contra Code: Up, up, down, down, left, right, left, right. After a mid-May toe injury, followed by Robinson Cano's suspension, the experiment was tabled, and Gordon returned to the keystone, where he proceeded to put up the worst full offensive season of his career.

Always a low walk, BABIP-dependent offensive profile, Gordon spent the summer of 2018 attempting to reach the limits of the hacky slap-hitter profile, setting a career high in swinging outside the zone and a career low in making contact out there. What he found at the edge of that space was a black hole, a .268 batting average, and the lowest walk rate of any qualified hitter in decades. After the addition of Mallex Smith and departure of Cano, Gordon's spot is as secure as any in the lineup. Given his track record, and historically late-aging skillset, he seems a relatively safe bet for a significant bounce back in 2019.

YEAR	TEAM	LVL	AGE	PA	DRC+	VORP	BABIP	BRR	FRAA	WARP
2016	MIA	MLB	28	345	72	7.2	.319	3.4	2B(78): -6.3	-0.4
2017	MIA	MLB	29	695	87	26.7	.354	8.4	2B(153): -0.6, SS(3): 0.0	1.8
2018	SEA	MLB	30	588	76	5.0	.304	4.2	2B(81): 2.5, CF(53): 0.7	0.9
2019	SEA	MLB	31	543	82	11.7	.308	4.3	2B -3, CF 0	0.8

Dee Gordon, continued

Batted Ball Distribution

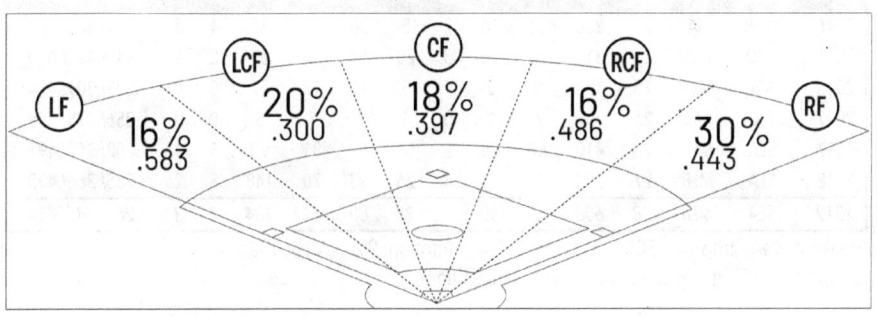

Strike Zone vs LHP   **Strike Zone vs RHP**

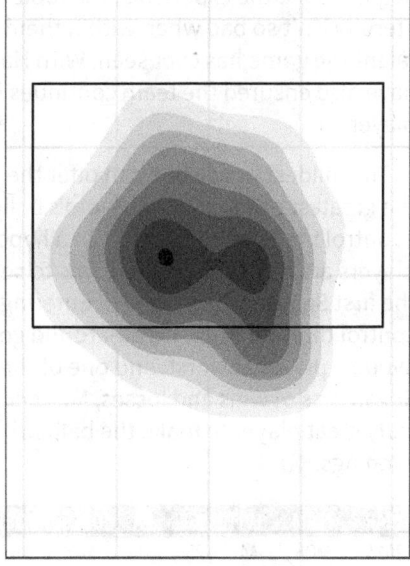

Mitch Haniger RF

Born: 12/23/90 Age: 28 Bats: R Throws: R
Height: 6'2" Weight: 215 Origin: Round 1, 2012 Draft (#38 overall)

YEAR	TEAM	LVL	AGE	PA	R	2B	3B	HR	RBI	BB	K	SB	CS	AVG/OBP/SLG
2016	MOB	AA	25	236	21	14	2	5	30	30	37	4	3	.294/.407/.462
2016	RNO	AAA	25	312	58	20	3	20	64	39	62	8	1	.341/.428/.670
2016	ARI	MLB	25	123	9	2	1	5	17	12	27	0	0	.229/.309/.404
2017	TAC	AAA	26	48	6	2	0	3	6	7	5	0	0	.256/.375/.538
2017	SEA	MLB	26	410	58	25	2	16	47	31	93	5	4	.282/.352/.491
2018	SEA	MLB	27	683	90	38	4	26	93	70	148	8	2	.285/.366/.493
2019	SEA	MLB	28	608	76	30	3	22	80	61	134	7	3	.263/.347/.454

Breakout: 3% Improve: 50% Collapse: 12% Attrition: 9% MLB: 100%
Comparables: Shin-Soo Choo, Matt Joyce, Kole Calhoun

Mediocrity has been a constant for Mariner fans, but a steady stream of superstar talent has, since the arrival of Ken Griffey Jr. in 1989, through Randy Johnson, Alex Rodriguez, Ichiro, Adrian Beltre, and finally Felix Hernandez, helped make the experience tolerable. Seventy-six wins or so a year for all eternity isn't so bad when within them flickers some of the greatest individual talent the game has ever seen. With Haniger's acquisition in 2016, Dipoto may have also ensured the team continues its run of having at least one truly elite player.

The mildest praise one can offer the Mariners' right fielder is that he is, by far, the greatest proponent of Dipoto's ballyhooed and seemingly disregarded "Control the Zone" approach. In a hypothetical fantasy draft, where all MLB players are available for all teams to select, Haniger would almost certainly be the first Seattle player picked. Entering his age-28 season, and under club control through 2022, his all-around good-to-great game renders him an above-average player at worst, and one of the game's best outfielders at best. Regardless of wins and losses, Mariner fans have a good chance of at least one truly great player to make the ballpark an enjoyable place to spend summer evenings.

YEAR	TEAM	LVL	AGE	PA	DRC+	VORP	BABIP	BRR	FRAA	WARP
2016	MOB	AA	25	236	142	17.9	.340	-0.9	LF(32): 1.4, CF(16): -0.4	1.4
2016	RNO	AAA	25	312	191	43.5	.373	3.4	RF(34): 3.3, CF(34): -0.4	3.9
2016	ARI	MLB	25	123	95	2.3	.256	0.2	CF(22): 1.5, LF(9): 0.1	0.5
2017	TAC	AAA	26	48	131	6.3	.219	-1.0	RF(6): 1.4	0.2
2017	SEA	MLB	26	410	115	16.8	.338	-1.4	RF(94): 4.7, CF(6): 0.2	2.0
2018	SEA	MLB	27	683	129	49.3	.336	-3.5	RF(144): 5.0, CF(35): -2.8	3.9
2019	SEA	MLB	28	608	121	32.5	.311	-0.4	RF 4, CF -1	3.6

Mitch Haniger, continued

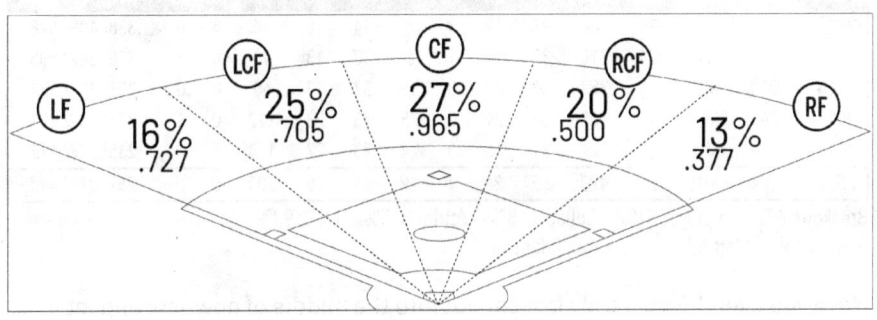

Batted Ball Distribution

Strike Zone vs LHP   **Strike Zone vs RHP**

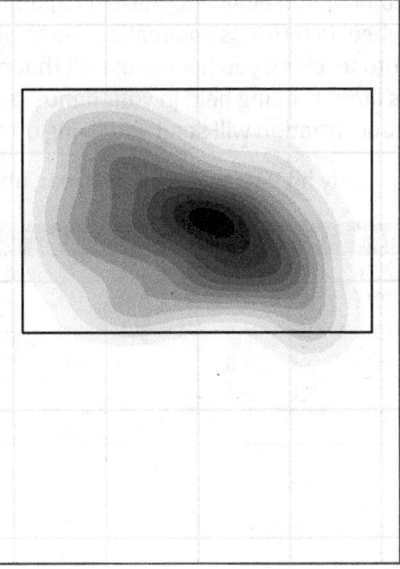

Seattle Mariners 2019

Ryon Healy 1B

Born: 01/10/92 Age: 27 Bats: R Throws: R
Height: 6'5" Weight: 225 Origin: Round 3, 2013 Draft (#100 overall)

YEAR	TEAM	LVL	AGE	PA	R	2B	3B	HR	RBI	BB	K	SB	CS	AVG/OBP/SLG
2016	MID	AA	24	164	27	12	3	8	34	18	35	1	0	.338/.409/.628
2016	NAS	AAA	24	210	33	16	1	6	30	13	40	0	1	.318/.362/.505
2016	OAK	MLB	24	283	36	20	0	13	37	12	60	0	0	.305/.337/.524
2017	OAK	MLB	25	605	66	29	0	25	78	23	142	0	1	.271/.302/.451
2018	SEA	MLB	26	524	51	15	0	24	73	27	113	0	0	.235/.277/.412
2019	SEA	MLB	27	493	55	24	1	19	65	29	108	0	0	.262/.310/.443

Breakout: 6% Improve: 51% Collapse: 8% Attrition: 5% MLB: 93%
Comparables: Matt Adams, C.J. Cron, Adam Lind

Have you ever driven a truly fast car out into the middle of nowhere and let it eat? Just settled that bad boy on a level, straight, empty stretch of road and punched the gas? Did you feel that sudden jolt of terror as you realized all the millions of man-hours and expertise that have gone into developing the combustion engine to make it capable of such pure savagery? Did you grip the wheel in terror as you realized none of those man-hours, not even one, went into teaching you how to use all that power the slightest bit? That your very life is literally being held in your hands, and the slightest miscalculation or lapse in concentration will send you flying off the road?

Healy hit 24 home runs last year, and had a lower DRC+ than Alex Gordon.

YEAR	TEAM	LVL	AGE	PA	DRC+	VORP	BABIP	BRR	FRAA	WARP
2016	MID	AA	24	164	173	18.5	.398	-0.5	1B(25): 0.5, 3B(7): -0.5	1.1
2016	NAS	AAA	24	210	141	17.5	.369	0.0	1B(19): -1.2, 3B(15): -3.5	0.5
2016	OAK	MLB	24	283	120	19.0	.352	-2.4	3B(72): -0.2	1.4
2017	OAK	MLB	25	605	98	5.5	.319	-2.1	1B(39): 0.9, 3B(34): -1.4	0.7
2018	SEA	MLB	26	524	93	-4.9	.257	-2.9	1B(131): -4.3, 3B(2): 0.0	-0.5
2019	SEA	MLB	27	493	100	8.7	.303	-1.0	1B -1, 3B -1	0.7

Ryon Healy, continued

Batted Ball Distribution

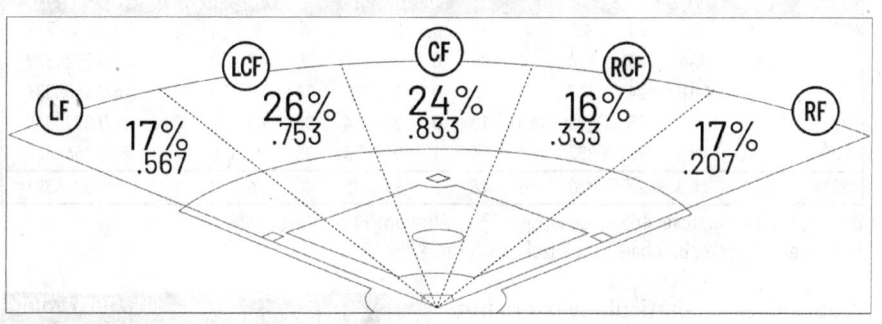

Strike Zone vs LHP **Strike Zone vs RHP**

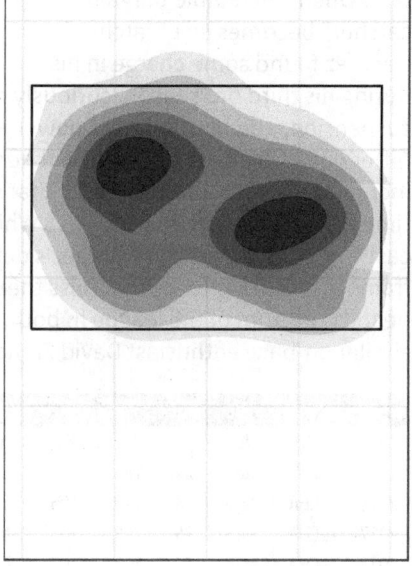

Omar Narvaez C

Born: 02/10/92   Age: 27   Bats: L   Throws: R
Height: 5'11"   Weight: 220   Origin: International Free Agent, 2008

YEAR	TEAM	LVL	AGE	PA	R	2B	3B	HR	RBI	BB	K	SB	CS	AVG/OBP/SLG
2016	BIR	AA	24	49	4	2	0	0	5	4	8	0	0	.222/.286/.267
2016	CHR	AAA	24	156	14	6	0	2	11	9	17	0	0	.245/.292/.329
2016	CHA	MLB	24	117	13	4	0	1	10	14	14	0	0	.267/.350/.337
2017	CHA	MLB	25	295	23	10	0	2	14	38	45	0	0	.277/.373/.340
2018	CHA	MLB	26	322	30	14	1	9	30	38	65	0	2	.275/.366/.429
2019	SEA	MLB	27	420	43	18	2	9	45	40	76	1	1	.259/.334/.391

Breakout: 3%   Improve: 46%   Collapse: 11%   Attrition: 11%   MLB: 99%
Comparables: Tucker Barnhart, Kurt Suzuki, Josh Thole

It doesn't seem particularly fair to fret over an on-base machine catcher once available in the minor league phase of the Rule 5 draft, but there comes a time when "incredible bargain catcher" becomes just "catcher." Narvaez found some charge in his bat during his third pro season, curiously right in line with Welington Castillo's PED suspension, and his moderate power and eagle eye combined to make the lefty hitter one of the best offensive catchers in the American League. (Note incredibly low bar, but proceed.) That's an impressive down payment on a long-time starting catcher, but the 2018 White Sox pitching staff was not the sort of cast that was going to let Narvaez's defensive flaws go unexposed. It's hard to frame and block pitches that miss their spots by feet, but Narvaez graded out near the bottom of the league in both, and this means he'll likely split time with similar on-base enthusiast David Freitas next year.

YEAR	TEAM	P. COUNT	FRM RUNS	BLK RUNS	THRW RUNS	TOT RUNS
2016	CHA	4399	-1.0	-0.8	-1.0	-2.9
2017	CHA	11422	-6.3	-1.5	-0.6	-9.3
2018	CHA	11231	-10.8	-4.6	-0.1	-15.7
2019	SEA	16539	-12.4	-3.5	-0.2	-16.1

YEAR	TEAM	LVL	AGE	PA	DRC+	VORP	BABIP	BRR	FRAA	WARP
2016	BIR	AA	24	49	80	-1.6	.270	-1.1	C(13): -0.2	-0.1
2016	CHR	AAA	24	156	76	0.1	.264	1.5	C(39): -4.4	-0.2
2016	CHA	MLB	24	117	105	5.0	.295	-0.5	C(34): -3.5	0.2
2017	CHA	MLB	25	295	100	8.2	.330	-1.0	C(83): -9.5, 1B(1): 0.0	0.4
2018	CHA	MLB	26	322	109	21.3	.330	0.0	C(85): -17.6	0.0
2019	SEA	MLB	27	420	96	17.7	.296	-0.8	C -20	-0.5

Omar Narvaez, continued

Batted Ball Distribution

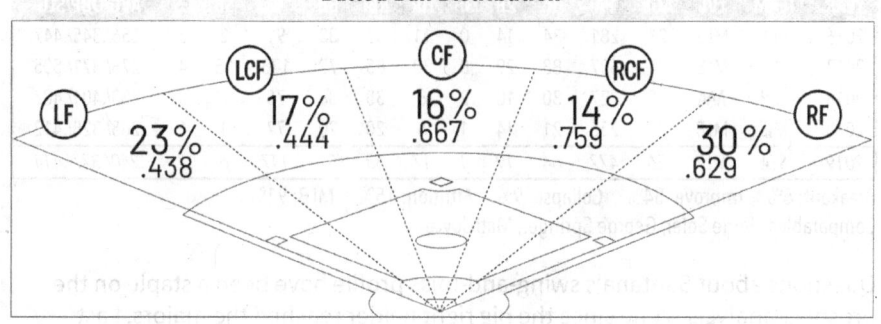

Strike Zone vs LHP

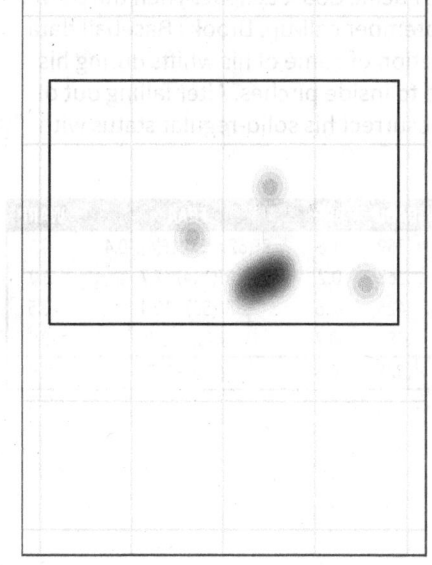

Strike Zone vs RHP

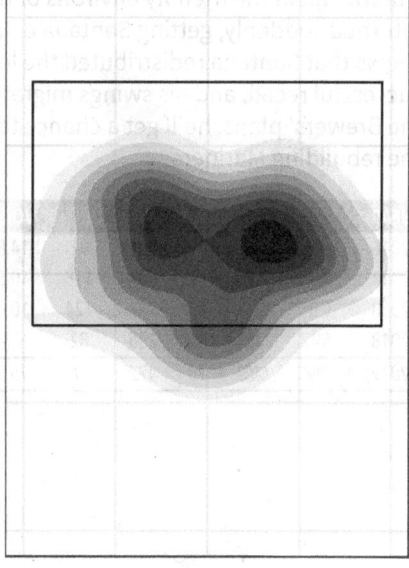

Domingo Santana LF

Born: 08/05/92 Age: 26 Bats: R Throws: R
Height: 6'5" Weight: 220 Origin: International Free Agent, 2009

YEAR	TEAM	LVL	AGE	PA	R	2B	3B	HR	RBI	BB	K	SB	CS	AVG/OBP/SLG
2016	MIL	MLB	23	281	34	14	0	11	32	32	91	2	3	.256/.345/.447
2017	MIL	MLB	24	607	88	29	0	30	85	73	178	15	4	.278/.371/.505
2018	CSP	AAA	25	227	30	10	2	8	35	36	75	2	0	.283/.401/.487
2018	MIL	MLB	25	235	21	14	1	5	20	20	77	1	1	.265/.328/.412
2019	SEA	MLB	26	472	64	19	1	17	53	51	147	6	2	.240/.327/.414

Breakout: 6% Improve: 54% Collapse: 9% Attrition: 15% MLB: 91%
Comparables: Jorge Soler, George Springer, Matt Joyce

Questions about Santana's swing-and-miss profile have been a staple on the prospect analysis scene since the big right fielder reached the majors. Last season was an adventure back to those questions, as Santana struck out in 33 percent of his plate appearances without doing much else during his first MLB stint, earning a demotion to Triple-A. It took another 17 games for Santana to hit a home run in the friendly environs of the Pacific Coast League. Then the power returned suddenly, getting Santana a September call-up. Brooks Baseball data shows that Santana redistributed the location of some of his whiffs during his successful recall, and his swings migrated to inside pitches. After falling out of the Brewers' plans, he'll get a chance to resurrect his solid-regular status with the rebuilding Mariners.

YEAR	TEAM	LVL	AGE	PA	DRC+	VORP	BABIP	BRR	FRAA	WARP
2016	MIL	MLB	23	281	91	14.8	.359	1.6	RF(62): -5.0, LF(4): -0.4	-0.1
2017	MIL	MLB	24	607	118	40.5	.363	0.2	RF(144): -7.7	2.0
2018	CSP	AAA	25	227	124	10.8	.425	-2.6	RF(50): -10.4	-0.5
2018	MIL	MLB	25	235	82	9.5	.386	-0.2	RF(55): -2.0	-0.2
2019	SEA	MLB	26	472	103	16.5	.329	-0.3	LF -5, RF -2	0.8

Domingo Santana, continued

Batted Ball Distribution

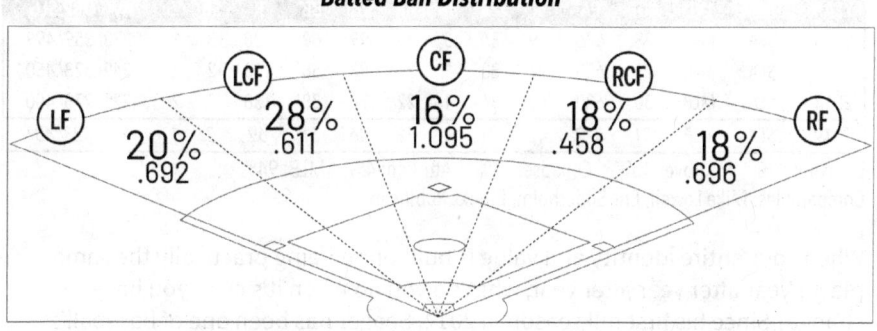

Strike Zone vs LHP

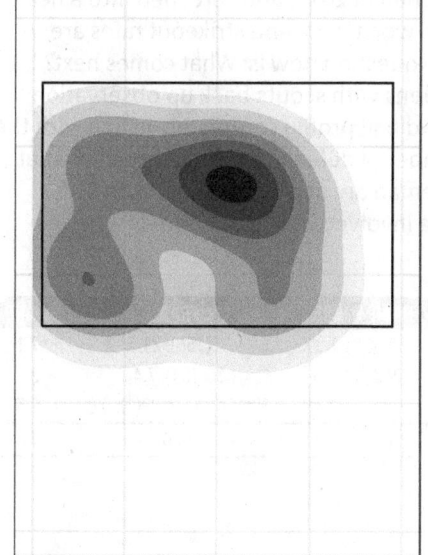

Strike Zone vs RHP

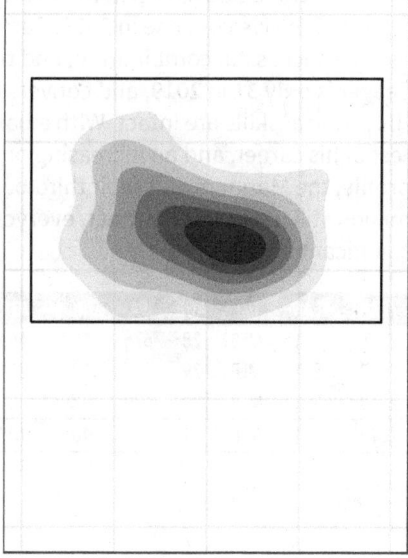

Kyle Seager 3B

Born: 11/03/87   Age: 31   Bats: L   Throws: R
Height: 6'0"   Weight: 210   Origin: Round 3, 2009 Draft (#82 overall)

YEAR	TEAM	LVL	AGE	PA	R	2B	3B	HR	RBI	BB	K	SB	CS	AVG/OBP/SLG
2016	SEA	MLB	28	676	89	36	3	30	99	69	108	3	1	.278/.359/.499
2017	SEA	MLB	29	650	72	33	1	27	88	58	110	2	1	.249/.323/.450
2018	SEA	MLB	30	630	62	36	1	22	78	38	138	2	2	.221/.273/.400
2019	SEA	MLB	31	372	42	21	1	12	46	31	69	2	1	.254/.323/.431

Breakout: 2%   Improve: 40%   Collapse: 17%   Attrition: 4%   MLB: 94%
Comparables: Mike Lowell, Eric Soderholm, Brooks Robinson

When your entire identity and value is built upon being practically the same player year after year after year, what do you do when it's clear you have to change? Since his first full season in 2012, Seager has been one of baseball's most dependable second-level stars, good for 25+ home runs, and solid-to-great defense at third base. He's also been remarkably durable, having never played in fewer than 154 games in a full season. That foundational dependability began to erode with a bad slump in the second half of 2017, and careened into a near full-on offensive collapse in 2018. Career-worst walk and strikeout rates are rarely a successful combination, and the question now is: What comes next? Seager is only 31 in 2019, and conversations with scouts back up observation: His physical skills are intact. With a batted ball profile completely in line with the rest of his career, and an increasing number of defensive shifts that nullify that profile, the Mariners and their third baseman are at a crossroads. With $58 million still left on his contract, everyone involved needs to hope for a significant bounceback.

YEAR	TEAM	LVL	AGE	PA	DRC+	VORP	BABIP	BRR	FRAA	WARP
2016	SEA	MLB	28	676	128	46.5	.295	1.8	3B(156): 21.5	7.1
2017	SEA	MLB	29	650	106	21.1	.262	-5.6	3B(154): 7.4	3.0
2018	SEA	MLB	30	630	90	8.1	.251	-1.6	3B(154): 11.2, 2B(1): 0.0	2.5
2019	SEA	MLB	31	372	104	10.2	.285	-0.7	3B 6	1.6

Kyle Seager, continued

Batted Ball Distribution

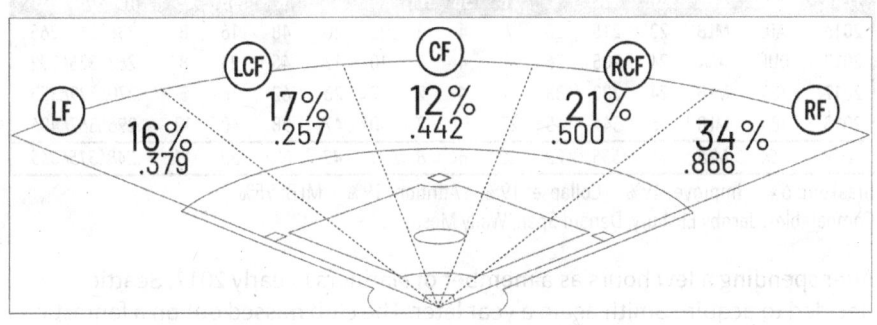

Strike Zone vs LHP   **Strike Zone vs RHP**

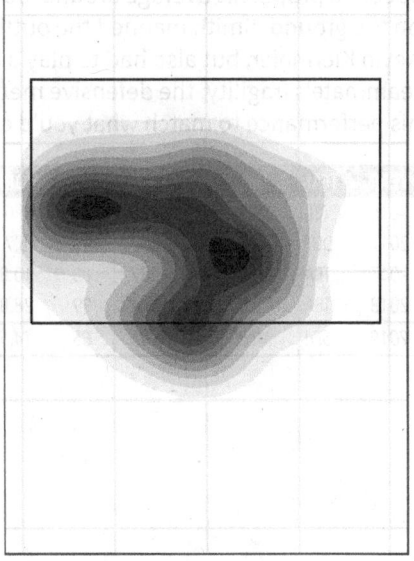

Mallex Smith OF

Born: 05/06/93   Age: 26   Bats: L   Throws: R
Height: 5'10"   Weight: 180   Origin: Round 5, 2012 Draft (#165 overall)

YEAR	TEAM	LVL	AGE	PA	R	2B	3B	HR	RBI	BB	K	SB	CS	AVG/OBP/SLG
2016	ATL	MLB	23	215	28	7	4	3	22	20	48	16	8	.238/.316/.365
2017	DUR	AAA	24	205	26	7	4	3	10	17	45	21	8	.263/.325/.392
2017	TBA	MLB	24	282	33	8	4	2	12	23	62	16	5	.270/.329/.355
2018	TBA	MLB	25	544	65	27	10	2	40	47	98	40	12	.296/.367/.406
2019	SEA	MLB	26	535	72	20	6	8	41	42	110	33	11	.248/.315/.365

Breakout: 6%   Improve: 49%   Collapse: 19%   Attrition: 19%   MLB: 95%
Comparables: Jacoby Ellsbury, Denard Span, Wally Moses

After spending a few hours as a member of Mariners in early 2017, Seattle decided to acquire Smith again a year later. The club missed out on a fantastic season that saw Smith become one of the more dynamic offensive players in the American League. He led the league with 10 triples and finished second behind Whit Merrifield with 40 steals. He showed good plate discipline and used his speed to propel his average around .300 despite hitting half of his balls in play on the ground. Smith manned the outfield corners most days, playing alongside Kevin Kiermaier, but also had to play a lot of center field due to his former teammate's fragility; the defensive metrics, FRAA in particular, didn't consider his performance to match what you'd expect from his tools.

YEAR	TEAM	LVL	AGE	PA	DRC+	VORP	BABIP	BRR	FRAA	WARP
2016	ATL	MLB	23	215	71	5.0	.302	0.2	CF(35): 2.9, LF(22): 0.2	0.2
2017	DUR	AAA	24	205	90	5.7	.333	2.3	CF(33): 5.1, LF(7): 0.5	0.8
2017	TBA	MLB	24	282	83	10.8	.347	2.1	CF(51): -5.2, LF(24): 0.2	0.1
2018	TBA	MLB	25	544	99	28.8	.366	4.4	CF(71): -7.0, RF(47): -1.9	0.9
2019	SEA	MLB	26	535	85	14.5	.300	3.6	CF -5	1.0

Mallex Smith, continued

Batted Ball Distribution

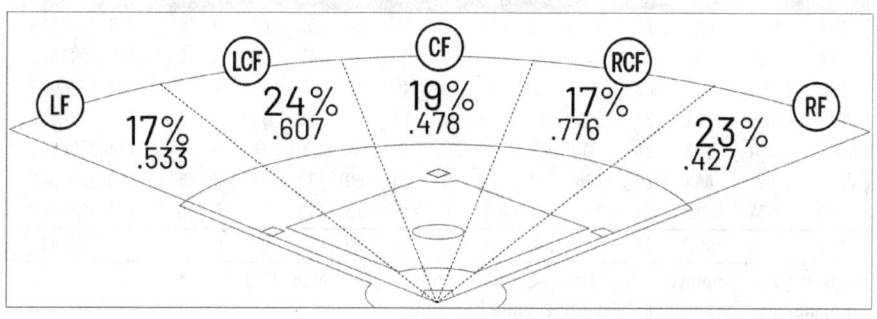

Strike Zone vs LHP   **Strike Zone vs RHP**

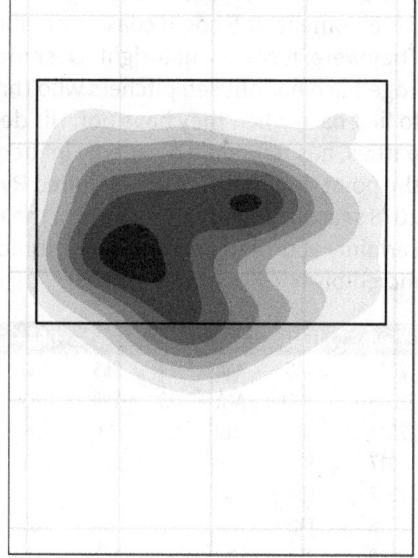

Dan Vogelbach 1B

Born: 12/17/92   Age: 26   Bats: L   Throws: R
Height: 6'0"   Weight: 250   Origin: Round 2, 2011 Draft (#68 overall)

YEAR	TEAM	LVL	AGE	PA	R	2B	3B	HR	RBI	BB	K	SB	CS	AVG/OBP/SLG
2016	IOW	AAA	23	365	53	18	2	16	64	55	67	0	0	.318/.425/.548
2016	TAC	AAA	23	198	26	7	0	7	32	42	34	0	0	.240/.404/.422
2016	SEA	MLB	23	13	0	0	0	0	0	1	6	0	0	.083/.154/.083
2017	TAC	AAA	24	541	65	25	0	17	83	76	98	3	1	.290/.388/.455
2017	SEA	MLB	24	31	0	1	0	0	2	3	9	0	0	.214/.290/.250
2018	TAC	AAA	25	378	54	16	0	20	60	77	59	0	1	.290/.434/.545
2018	SEA	MLB	25	102	9	2	0	4	13	13	26	0	0	.207/.324/.368
2019	SEA	MLB	26	160	20	6	0	6	20	22	34	0	0	.235/.344/.412

Breakout: 5%   Improve: 45%   Collapse: 6%   Attrition: 28%   MLB: 71%
Comparables: Kila Ka'aihue, Tyler White, Vince Belnome

The Mariners traded for Vogelbach late in 2016 believing two things: Firstly, that his polished, disciplined approach at the plate and unique frame could translate into an above-average offensive bat, and secondly, that their player development staff could coax a passable defensive first basemen out of him. They were, it seems, half-right. Over more than two seasons in Triple-A Tacoma, Vogelbach has abused pitchers who throw him strikes, and been content to lope to first base when they have not. His defense, despite sincere effort from all parties, has remained decidedly inadequate, if not quite at Dae-Ho Lee levels, to the point that the Mariners acquired Ryon Healy (on purpose even!) before the 2018 season. Vogelbach's future in the majors, if he is to have one, is almost certainly at designated hitter. The rumors, it turns out, are true. First base is incredibly hard.

YEAR	TEAM	LVL	AGE	PA	DRC+	VORP	BABIP	BRR	FRAA	WARP
2016	IOW	AAA	23	365	160	35.7	.362	-1.8	1B(76): -3.0	1.7
2016	TAC	AAA	23	198	163	8.9	.263	-3.1	1B(25): -0.9	0.8
2016	SEA	MLB	23	13	64	-2.3	.167	-0.4	1B(4): -0.3	-0.1
2017	TAC	AAA	24	541	123	20.9	.332	-7.3	1B(81): -8.3	-0.1
2017	SEA	MLB	24	31	82	-3.0	.316	-1.2	1B(7): -0.3	-0.2
2018	TAC	AAA	25	378	165	27.8	.299	-6.0	1B(53): -2.9	1.8
2018	SEA	MLB	25	102	92	1.0	.246	0.6	1B(20): -1.1	0.0
2019	SEA	MLB	26	160	110	4.7	.274	-0.3	1B -2	0.3

Dan Vogelbach, continued

Batted Ball Distribution

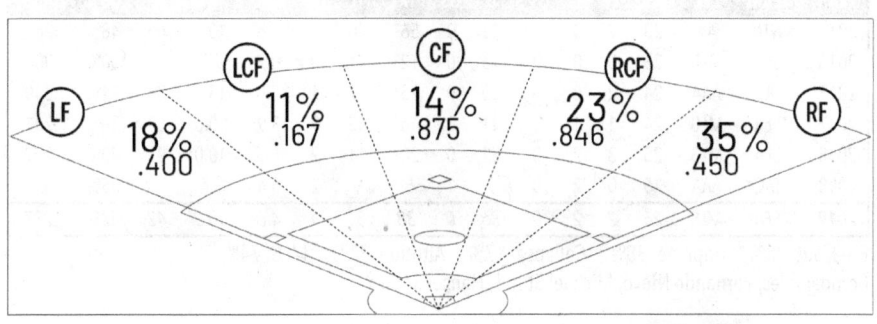

Strike Zone vs LHP   **Strike Zone vs RHP**

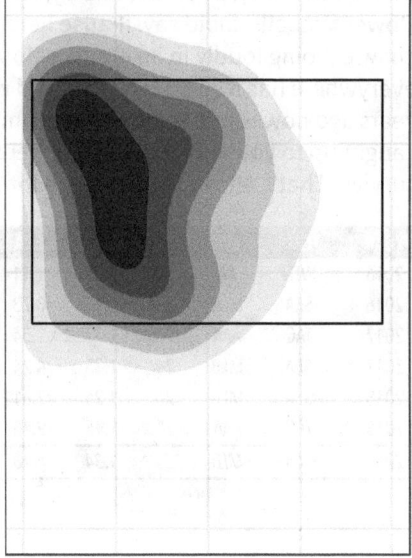

Seattle Mariners 2019

Dan Altavilla RHP

Born: 09/08/92 Age: 26 Bats: R Throws: R
Height: 5'11" Weight: 200 Origin: Round 5, 2014 Draft (#141 overall)

YEAR	TEAM	LVL	AGE	W	L	SV	G	GS	IP	H	HR	BB/9	K/9	K	GB%	BABIP
2016	WTN	AA	23	7	3	16	43	0	56²	40	3	3.5	10.3	65	48%	.261
2016	SEA	MLB	23	0	0	0	15	0	12¹	11	0	0.7	7.3	10	50%	.306
2017	TAC	AAA	24	2	0	6	20	0	23¹	17	1	5.8	13.9	36	44%	.340
2017	SEA	MLB	24	1	1	0	41	0	46²	43	9	3.9	10.0	52	38%	.281
2018	SEA	MLB	25	3	2	0	22	0	20²	11	2	6.5	10.0	23	40%	.209
2018	TAC	AAA	25	0	2	0	9	1	6²	9	2	5.4	9.4	7	35%	.333
2019	SEA	MLB	26	2	2	0	36	0	38	31	4	4.6	10.0	42	42%	.287

Breakout: 28% Improve: 38% Collapse: 17% Attrition: 21% MLB: 74%
Comparables: Fernando Nieve, Michael Stutes, Hansel Robles

It's a hard fact of life that things change. It used to be when a fella had a fastball that averaged 96 mph and a slider that moved through the multiverse on its way to home, he could count on them. Getting through life one eighth inning at a time wasn't easy, but it got one by, and that was more than many relievers with slower fastballs could say. (Pause here to spit dramatically into a spittoon, the chaw echoing loudly in an empty saloon.) These days, though, seems everybody everywhere has a 96 mph heater, and what made someone like Altavilla a few years ago now is just keeping him from being left behind. When the world's caught up to you and you're no longer special, the real trick is learning to survive. That's Altavilla's challenge for 2019.

YEAR	TEAM	LVL	AGE	WHIP	ERA	DRA	WARP	MPH	FB%	WHF	CSP
2016	WTN	AA	23	1.09	1.91	3.63	0.7				
2016	SEA	MLB	23	0.97	0.73	3.38	0.2	99.2	66.3	12.8	53.3
2017	TAC	AAA	24	1.37	1.54	2.26	0.8				
2017	SEA	MLB	24	1.35	4.24	3.88	0.7	98.8	62.4	13.9	48.5
2018	SEA	MLB	25	1.26	2.61	3.45	0.4	98.4	52.8	13.4	44.3
2018	TAC	AAA	25	1.95	9.45	2.97	0.2				
2019	SEA	MLB	26	1.34	4.18	4.42	0.3	98.3	60.7	13.9	48.8

Dan Altavilla, continued

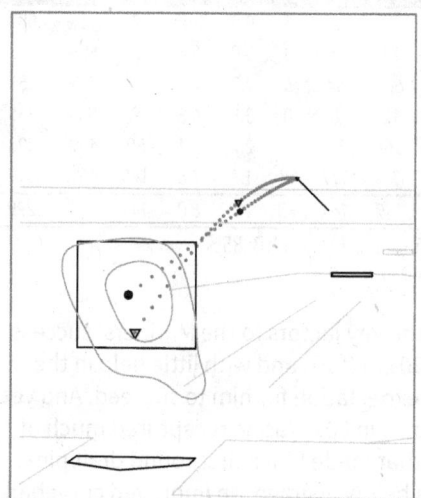

Pitch Shape vs LHH

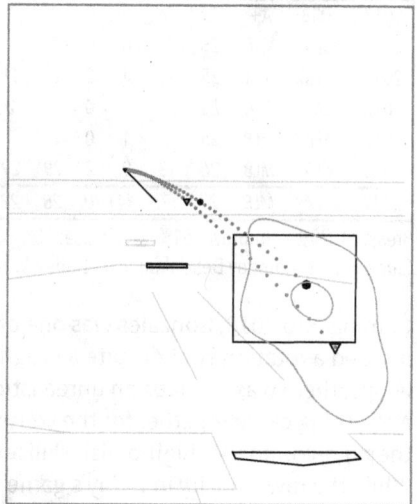

Pitch Shape vs RHH

Type	Frequency	Velocity	H Movement	V Movement
● Fastball	52.8%	96.6 [113]	-8.2 [93]	-12.5 [110]
☐ Sinker				
+ Cutter				
▲ Changeup	0.3%	90.6 [121]	-11 [101]	-19.9 [122]
✕ Splitter				
▽ Slider	46.9%	88 [116]	6.8 [109]	-28.5 [113]
◇ Curveball				
⊕ Slow Curveball				
✳ Knuckleball				
▼ Screwball				

Marco Gonzales   LHP

Born: 02/16/92   Age: 27   Bats: L   Throws: L
Height: 6'1"   Weight: 195   Origin: Round 1, 2013 Draft (#19 overall)

YEAR	TEAM	LVL	AGE	W	L	SV	G	GS	IP	H	HR	BB/9	K/9	K	GB%	BABIP
2017	PMB	A+	25	0	0	0	1	1	6	2	1	0.0	10.5	7	38%	.083
2017	SLN	MLB	25	0	0	0	1	1	3^1	6	3	0.0	5.4	2	50%	.273
2017	MEM	AAA	25	6	4	0	11	11	68^1	54	6	2.2	7.5	57	45%	.255
2017	TAC	AAA	25	2	0	0	2	2	12	8	0	3.8	6.8	9	56%	.235
2017	SEA	MLB	25	1	1	0	10	7	36^2	53	5	2.7	7.4	30	45%	.393
2018	SEA	MLB	26	13	9	0	29	29	166^2	172	17	1.7	7.8	145	45%	.319
2019	SEA	MLB	27	9	11	0	28	28	159	161	23	2.5	8.0	141	45%	.299

Breakout: 28%   Improve: 61%   Collapse: 10%   Attrition: 11%   MLB: 85%
Comparables: Anthony DeSclafani, Tyler Duffey, Wade Miley

Coming into 2018, Gonzales was one of the key factors to the Mariners' success: handed a rotation spot despite a rough 2017 effort, and with little help in the wings, there was perhaps an unrealistic expectation for him to succeed. And yet everything came together for the southpaw in 2018, as he recaptured much of the high-command, high-polish skillset that made him a first-round draft pick. While the raw velocity in today's game is below average, an improved curveball coupled with the addition of a superb cutter (unavailable while recovering from Tommy John) resulted in exactly the mid-rotation performance Jerry Dipoto envisioned when he acquired him from St. Louis in 2017. While it's fair to question whether Gonzales' ceiling is much higher than what he showed last year, for an organization as thin in pitching as Seattle, they will happily take an approximate repeat of 2018 next year. If healthy, given his contract status, Mariner fans can hope for it for many more years than that.

YEAR	TEAM	LVL	AGE	WHIP	ERA	DRA	WARP	MPH	FB%	WHF	CSP
2017	PMB	A+	25	0.33	1.50	2.94	0.2				
2017	SLN	MLB	25	1.80	13.50	3.83	0.1	92.4	69	13.8	43
2017	MEM	AAA	25	1.04	2.90	3.67	1.5				
2017	TAC	AAA	25	1.08	4.50	3.28	0.3				
2017	SEA	MLB	25	1.75	5.40	4.51	0.4	93.1	51	9.8	44.5
2018	SEA	MLB	26	1.22	4.00	3.58	3.3	91.5	32.5	10.2	49.4
2019	SEA	MLB	27	1.30	4.32	4.64	1.4	91.3	36.5	10.3	47.7

Marco Gonzales, continued

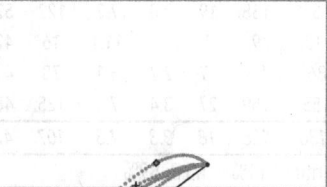
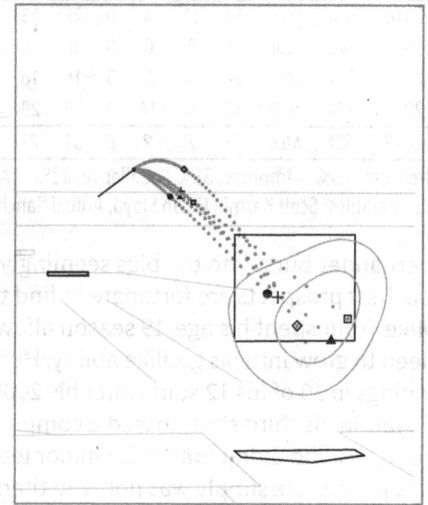

Type	Frequency	Velocity	H Movement	V Movement
● Fastball	9.1%	90.8 [95]	8.6 [91]	-15.5 [101]
□ Sinker	23.4%	90.7 [91]	13.4 [94]	-18.5 [106]
+ Cutter	22.2%	87.6 [93]	-0.9 [94]	-21.9 [107]
▲ Changeup	23.0%	84.2 [95]	15.9 [75]	-27.8 [99]
× Splitter				
▽ Slider				
◇ Curveball	22.3%	78.6 [100]	-6 [92]	-51.5 [92]
◈ Slow Curveball				
✳ Knuckleball				
▼ Screwball				

Felix Hernandez RHP

Born: 04/08/86   Age: 33   Bats: R   Throws: R
Height: 6'3"   Weight: 225   Origin: International Free Agent, 2002

YEAR	TEAM	LVL	AGE	W	L	SV	G	GS	IP	H	HR	BB/9	K/9	K	GB%	BABIP
2016	SEA	MLB	30	11	8	0	25	25	153^1	138	19	3.8	7.2	122	52%	.271
2017	TAC	AAA	31	2	0	0	3	3	13	9	1	2.1	11.1	16	42%	.267
2017	SEA	MLB	31	6	5	0	16	16	86^2	86	17	2.7	8.1	78	49%	.287
2018	SEA	MLB	32	8	14	0	29	28	155^2	159	27	3.4	7.2	125	48%	.286
2019	SEA	MLB	33	7	9	0	31	21	130	126	18	3.3	7.3	107	47%	.286

Breakout: 13%   Improve: 38%   Collapse: 23%   Attrition: 11%   MLB: 89%
Comparables: Scott Kazmir, Gavin Floyd, Anibal Sanchez

Hernandez burst into the bigs seemingly fully formed at 19, an age where even the best prospects are fortunate to find themselves in Double-A. While even Mike Trout spent his age-19 season allowing baseball the illusion that he would need to grow into his godlike ability, Hernandez did no such thing. He threw 7+ innings in 10 of his 12 starts after his 2005 callup. He struck out 11 against the Royals in his third start, tossed a complete game against Texas a month later. For a fan who didn't follow the minor leagues, there was no development for this pitcher. He simply was not, and then very much was.

The tragedies of Hernandez, then, are twofold. He has built a borderline Hall-of-Fame resume, and made hundreds of millions of dollars. He is one of the most successful, dynamic, beloved, memorable starters of his era. But he famously never played on a Mariner team that made the postseason. While no fault of his own, his career and our appreciation of it are lessened having never seen such an imposing ace toe the rubber in October.

More (or at least more presently) disappointing is the way in which Hernandez's career has fallen off. His age at the beginning of his career, combined with that seemingly unnecessary development period, allowed anyone interested in seeing a starting pitcher reach the counting totals of yesteryear's greats to hope. Could we see 300 wins? Top-10 in strikeouts? How many Cy Youngs? Anything seems possible when you're an ace by 23.

It's hard not to mourn for Hernandez's career. The decline was inevitable, if unscheduled. But the true greats are marked by an ability to gently glide downward during it, and Hernandez plummeted. He has lost his status as ace, team's best pitcher, quality major league starter, back end filler, competent major leaguer. In 2018 he was one of the worst starting pitchers in the game. He enters 2019, at 33—still so young for one who seems so old—in the final year of his contract. It's not hard to imagine where things go after this year, but it's entirely unpleasant. A kingdom mourns its once-mighty king.

YEAR	TEAM	LVL	AGE	WHIP	ERA	DRA	WARP	MPH	FB%	WHF	CSP
2016	SEA	MLB	30	1.32	3.82	5.74	-0.7	92.9	47	10.4	43.1
2017	TAC	AAA	31	0.92	4.15	3.13	0.4				
2017	SEA	MLB	31	1.29	4.36	5.72	-0.1	92.2	44.5	10.2	46.5
2018	SEA	MLB	32	1.40	5.55	5.30	0.0	91.1	43.3	8.8	45.3
2019	*SEA*	*MLB*	*33*	*1.32*	*4.70*	*5.01*	*0.6*	*90.9*	*44.1*	*9.4*	*44.6*

Seattle Mariners 2019

Felix Hernandez, continued

Pitch Shape vs LHH

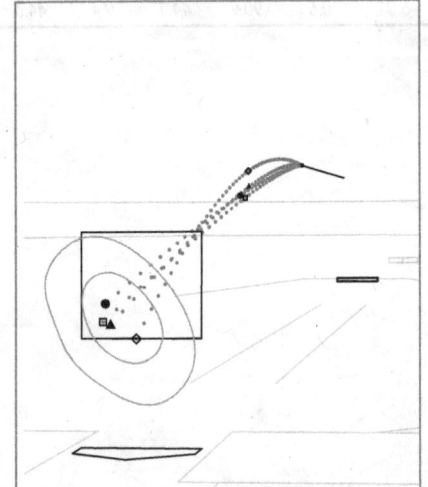

Pitch Shape vs RHH

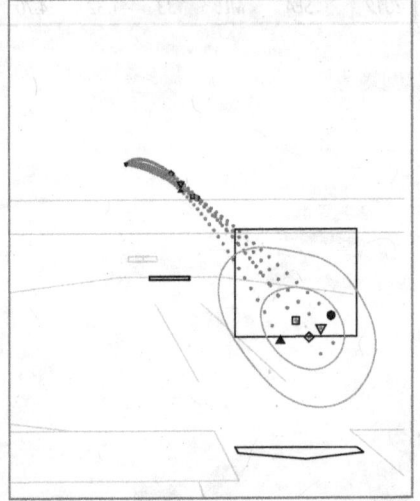

Type	Frequency	Velocity	H Movement	V Movement
● Fastball	9.6%	90.4 [93]	-3.5 [115]	-17.6 [94]
□ Sinker	33.0%	89.8 [87]	-11.3 [110]	-22.5 [93]
+ Cutter	0.6%	88.5 [98]	1.4 [97]	-23.3 [102]
▲ Changeup	24.1%	85.5 [101]	-8 [118]	-32 [86]
✕ Splitter				
▽ Slider	5.0%	82.4 [91]	6.4 [107]	-37.1 [88]
◇ Curveball	27.6%	79.4 [104]	9.7 [108]	-47.9 [100]
⊕ Slow Curveball	0.0%	72.4 [109]	14.7 [110]	-58.7 [109]
✱ Knuckleball				
▼ Screwball				

Mike Leake   RHP

Born: 11/12/87   Age: 31   Bats: R   Throws: R
Height: 5'10"   Weight: 170   Origin: Round 1, 2009 Draft (#8 overall)

YEAR	TEAM	LVL	AGE	W	L	SV	G	GS	IP	H	HR	BB/9	K/9	K	GB%	BABIP
2016	SLN	MLB	28	9	12	0	30	30	176²	203	20	1.5	6.4	125	55%	.318
2017	SLN	MLB	29	7	12	0	26	26	154	169	19	2.0	6.0	103	55%	.306
2017	SEA	MLB	29	3	1	0	5	5	32	32	1	0.6	7.6	27	50%	.323
2018	SEA	MLB	30	10	10	0	31	31	185²	207	23	1.6	5.8	119	50%	.306
2019	SEA	MLB	31	9	11	0	28	28	168	177	24	2.2	6.3	118	50%	.295

Breakout: 12%   Improve: 39%   Collapse: 29%   Attrition: 12%   MLB: 95%
Comparables: Joel Pineiro, Bob Friend, Ivan Nova

The oceans may rise, cities may fall, and fires may rain from the heavens. Still, there will be Leake. He will throw 170-200 innings. He will not allow walks, nor home runs. That is good because he will not get strikeouts. He will have two or three starts in a row where BABIP is friendly to him, and someone somewhere will write about him "taking his career to the next level". That notion will be disproved immediately, when the hits string together and he allows five or more runs in his next three starts. He will do this forever. Your children's children's children's great grandchildren will sit in their holoseats, and watch Leake go six and a third, allowing three runs, and striking out two. World without end. Amen.

YEAR	TEAM	LVL	AGE	WHIP	ERA	DRA	WARP	MPH	FB%	WHF	CSP
2016	SLN	MLB	28	1.32	4.69	3.43	3.9	93.0	77.4	7.6	46.9
2017	SLN	MLB	29	1.32	4.21	4.20	2.4	91.6	70.9	8.5	48.8
2017	SEA	MLB	29	1.06	2.53	3.64	0.7	92.1	70.9	9.7	47.9
2018	SEA	MLB	30	1.30	4.36	4.46	1.8	90.5	59.4	8.3	50.7
2019	SEA	MLB	31	1.31	4.55	4.89	1.0	90.7	67.2	8.2	48.8

Seattle Mariners 2019

Mike Leake, continued

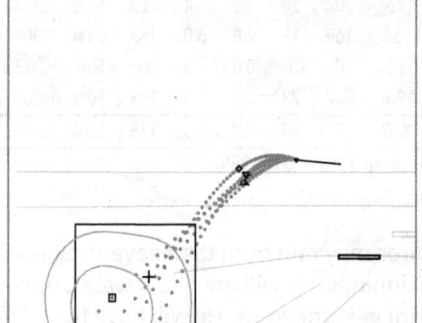
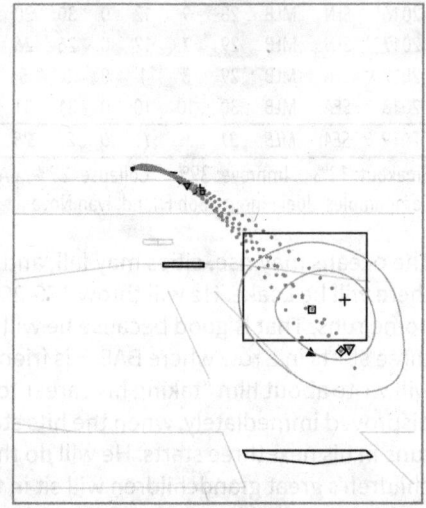

Type	Frequency	Velocity	H Movement	V Movement
● Fastball	0.9%	89.7 [91]	-7.4 [97]	-21.7 [81]
□ Sinker	36.2%	89.2 [84]	-11.2 [112]	-27.4 [77]
+ Cutter	22.3%	87.7 [93]	1 [95]	-25.4 [93]
▲ Changeup	18.6%	84.1 [95]	-11.7 [98]	-35 [77]
× Splitter				
▽ Slider	12.3%	80.5 [82]	8.8 [117]	-39.4 [81]
◇ Curveball	9.7%	78.7 [101]	13.4 [124]	-45.7 [105]
✜ Slow Curveball				
✳ Knuckleball				
▼ Screwball				

Wade LeBlanc   LHP

Born: 08/07/84   Age: 34   Bats: L   Throws: L
Height: 6'3"   Weight: 205   Origin: Round 2, 2006 Draft (#61 overall)

YEAR	TEAM	LVL	AGE	W	L	SV	G	GS	IP	H	HR	BB/9	K/9	K	GB%	BABIP
2016	BUF	AAA	31	7	2	0	14	14	89^2	84	3	2.1	8.5	85	43%	.315
2016	SEA	MLB	31	3	0	1	11	8	50	52	14	1.6	7.4	41	34%	.264
2016	PIT	MLB	31	1	0	1	8	0	12	7	0	1.5	7.5	10	41%	.219
2017	PIT	MLB	32	5	2	1	50	0	68	64	10	2.2	7.1	54	47%	.269
2018	SEA	MLB	33	9	5	0	32	27	162	151	24	2.2	7.2	130	37%	.273
2019	SEA	MLB	34	6	10	0	24	24	127	133	23	2.7	7.4	105	40%	.291

Breakout: 13%   Improve: 29%   Collapse: 21%   Attrition: 16%   MLB: 74%
Comparables: Eric Stults, Chris Narveson, Claudio Vargas

If you ever wanted an elevator pitch for caring about the game of baseball, you could do a lot worse than LeBlanc's 2018 season. After a decade hovering around the fringes of big league rosters as a near replacement-level pitcher, the soft-tossing lefty found unprecedented success in his second stint in Seattle. Posting a career high in innings and strikeouts, the Mariners rewarded LeBlanc with his first ever multi-year contract, a team option deal that could theoretically keep him in Seattle through 2022. So, how did he do it? How did a 33-year old man with an 86 mph fastball and ten seasons telling us he barely belonged in the league spend 166 innings surviving Mike Trout, Mookie Betts and the rest of the American League? Did he add a new pitch? A new windup that concealed the ball longer from the hitter? Combing the data, the answer seems to be: Nothing. LeBlanc threw the same pitch mix, at the same speed, from the same arm slots. Amazingly, most of his results were perfectly in line with career norms. He just... did them longer... and the results proved slightly better. He'll almost certainly never repeat last season, but that's not the point. By all accounts last season never should have happened in the first place. As analytics press us ever onward towards a fully optimized future, baseball's ability to still produce season-long accidents like LeBlanc's 2018 is something to cherish.

YEAR	TEAM	LVL	AGE	WHIP	ERA	DRA	WARP	MPH	FB%	WHF	CSP
2016	BUF	AAA	31	1.17	1.71	2.82	2.6				
2016	SEA	MLB	31	1.22	4.50	5.65	-0.2	89.0	62.9	10.1	46.7
2016	PIT	MLB	31	0.75	0.75	3.91	0.2	88.7	62.9	13.8	47.8
2017	PIT	MLB	32	1.19	4.50	3.77	1.1	88.4	62.9	10.3	46.1
2018	SEA	MLB	33	1.18	3.72	5.07	0.4	87.5	61.1	10.1	47.7
2019	SEA	MLB	34	1.34	4.99	5.36	0.1	86.8	60.8	10.1	46.2

Seattle Mariners 2019

Wade LeBlanc, continued

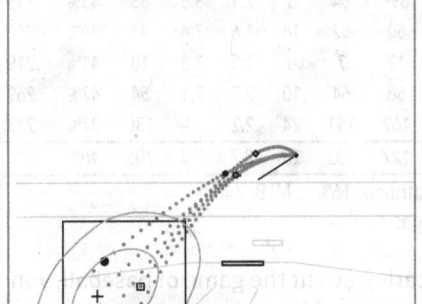
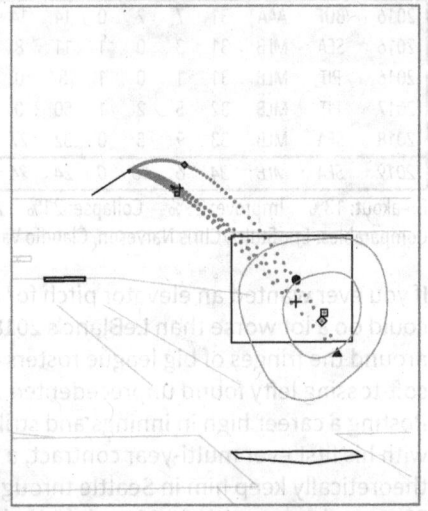

Type	Frequency	Velocity	H Movement	V Movement
● Fastball	8.6%	86.7 [81]	8.6 [91]	-19.1 [90]
☐ Sinker	27.1%	86.7 [72]	13.8 [90]	-22.9 [92]
+ Cutter	25.4%	83.8 [71]	-0.6 [93]	-25.8 [92]
▲ Changeup	29.8%	78.2 [72]	13 [91]	-34.6 [78]
✕ Splitter				
▽ Slider	0.1%	78.9 [75]	-5.2 [101]	-37.4 [87]
◇ Curveball	9.0%	72.9 [79]	-9.5 [107]	-52.8 [89]
✦ Slow Curveball				
✳ Knuckleball				
▼ Screwball				

54 - Mariners Player Analysis

Tommy Milone LHP

Born: 02/16/87 Age: 32 Bats: L Throws: L
Height: 6'0" Weight: 215 Origin: Round 10, 2008 Draft (#301 overall)

YEAR	TEAM	LVL	AGE	W	L	SV	G	GS	IP	H	HR	BB/9	K/9	K	GB%	BABIP
2016	ROC	AAA	29	4	0	0	7	7	48^2	41	4	0.7	7.6	41	43%	.268
2016	MIN	MLB	29	3	5	0	19	12	69^1	84	15	2.9	6.4	49	48%	.308
2017	MIL	MLB	30	1	0	1	6	3	21	29	6	0.9	6.9	16	35%	.333
2017	BIN	AA	30	1	0	0	4	4	20	26	8	0.9	4.9	11	27%	.273
2017	NYN	MLB	30	0	3	0	11	5	27^1	36	9	4.0	7.2	22	36%	.318
2018	SYR	AAA	31	7	4	0	20	20	109^2	101	11	2.0	9.3	113	36%	.303
2018	WAS	MLB	31	1	1	0	5	4	26^1	37	7	0.3	7.9	23	30%	.349
2019	SEA	MLB	32	5	7	0	19	19	102^1	105	20	2.8	7.9	90	39%	.288

Breakout: 21% Improve: 41% Collapse: 17% Attrition: 19% MLB: 69%
Comparables: Josh Towers, Zach Duke, Victor Santos

Things are trending against Milone, you might say. His major-league innings total sank by 21 from 2016 to 2017, then by 22 from 2017 to 2018. The advanced math thusly shows that Milone is projected to throw 3 1/3 innings in 2019. Though his peripherals haven't tanked as badly as some other very employed pitchers, you're probably better off if those innings aren't for your team. But if he does wind up on a mound you care about, at least you'll get that brief moment of hope that, hey, yes, tying your kid's right hand behind their back five days a week may still afford you an excellent retirement.

YEAR	TEAM	LVL	AGE	WHIP	ERA	DRA	WARP	MPH	FB%	WHF	CSP
2016	ROC	AAA	29	0.92	1.66	2.93	1.3				
2016	MIN	MLB	29	1.53	5.71	5.89	-0.5	89.7	54.5	9.5	44.2
2017	MIL	MLB	30	1.48	6.43	6.38	-0.2	89.1	65.2	8.3	43.8
2017	BIN	AA	30	1.40	4.95	4.72	0.1				
2017	NYN	MLB	30	1.76	8.56	5.28	0.1	89.0	65.2	8.9	42.5
2018	SYR	AAA	31	1.14	4.19	3.30	2.8				
2018	WAS	MLB	31	1.44	5.81	4.64	0.2	88.5	58.9	11.7	46.9
2019	SEA	MLB	32	1.34	5.21	5.60	-0.1	88.3	59	9.6	44.5

Seattle Mariners 2019

Tommy Milone, continued

Pitch Shape vs LHH

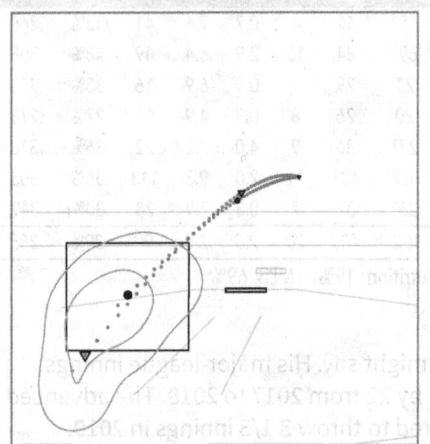

Pitch Shape vs RHH

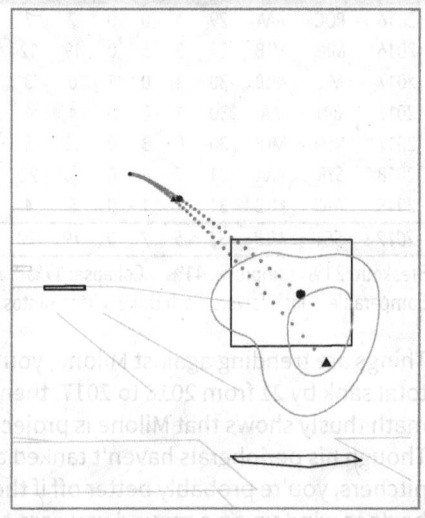

Type	Frequency	Velocity	H Movement	V Movement
● Fastball	54.5%	87.3 [83]	7 [98]	-16.5 [98]
□ Sinker				
+ Cutter	4.3%	84.9 [77]	2.7 [73]	-20.9 [111]
▲ Changeup	25.4%	78.9 [74]	12.4 [94]	-30.8 [90]
× Splitter				
▽ Slider	12.0%	78.4 [73]	-2.8 [91]	-39.8 [80]
◇ Curveball	3.8%	73.8 [83]	-3.8 [83]	-49.6 [96]
✦ Slow Curveball				
✱ Knuckleball				
▼ Screwball				

www.baseballprospectus.com

Hunter Strickland   RHP

Born: 09/24/88   Age: 30   Bats: R   Throws: R
Height: 6'3"   Weight: 225   Origin: Round 18, 2007 Draft (#564 overall)

YEAR	TEAM	LVL	AGE	W	L	SV	G	GS	IP	H	HR	BB/9	K/9	K	GB%	BABIP
2016	SFN	MLB	27	3	3	3	72	0	61	50	4	2.8	8.4	57	47%	.274
2017	SFN	MLB	28	4	3	1	68	0	61[1]	59	4	4.3	8.5	58	38%	.314
2018	SFN	MLB	29	3	5	14	49	0	45[1]	43	5	4.2	7.3	37	40%	.277
2019	SEA	MLB	30	2	3	20	52	0	54	51	7	3.9	8.1	49	42%	.284

Breakout: 25%   Improve: 52%   Collapse: 24%   Attrition: 12%   MLB: 92%
Comparables: Darren O'Day, Jason Frasor, Ramon Ramirez

The growth of social media has given fans a clearer window into players' lives away from the field than ever before in the game's history. Follow Strickland on Instagram, for instance, and you'll quickly learn that Hunter is, fittingly, an avid hunter who even created his own line of hunting gear. Stay a while, and you'll see pictures of his daughter, Kinsey, throwbacks to his high-school days in Georgia and, of course, his latest 10-point buck. But while it's increasingly hard for players to keep their private lives private, there's a lot about our favorite hitters and pitchers that we don't know until they tell us.

Strickland's anger issues are well documented, and they've boiled over twice in as many seasons. First, there was the culmination of his long-held grudge against Bryce Harper; then there was his losing battle against a dugout door. Those blow-ups have cost the right-hander his reputation, the closer role and two months of the 2018 season. And through all that, he kept a secret.

Last September, Strickland finally revealed that he's spent two years battling ulcerative colitis, cycling through myriad medications that contributed to his fits of rage. He opened up about the condition not to beg for sympathy, but to use his platform to help others afflicted by the same disease. The pain and frustration that come with colitis excuse neither Strickland's behavior nor the dip in his performance. But they do lend context to both, and perspective for those who ripped him on talk radio or Twitter without knowing all the facts.

Strickland's season began with saves in consecutive 1-0 wins over the Dodgers. He was throwing his slider with more conviction after seeking John Smoltz's advice in the offseason, and collecting more whiffs on the breaking ball as a result. Then, after a meltdown in June, he broke his hand. Strickland's velocity and command weren't the same when he returned in August, and a year that started so brightly became a letdown, perhaps prompting his disclosure.

Whatever you now think of Strickland the pitcher—closer or righty specialist—or Strickland the person—real tough guy or fake—you can render a more informed verdict because he opened up. Other players may choose to keep their off-field matters and maladies to themselves. Before judging them, remember that there's usually more to the men than their work and antics on the field.

YEAR	TEAM	LVL	AGE	WHIP	ERA	DRA	WARP	MPH	FB%	WHF	CSP
2016	SFN	MLB	27	1.13	3.10	4.00	0.7	99.5	73.1	12.7	49.5
2017	SFN	MLB	28	1.43	2.64	5.11	0.0	97.5	68.5	11.7	49.2
2018	SFN	MLB	29	1.41	3.97	4.49	0.2	97.0	64.3	11.8	46.9
2019	SEA	MLB	30	1.35	4.64	4.78	0.2	97.1	68.1	12	48.2

Hunter Strickland, continued

Pitch Shape vs LHH

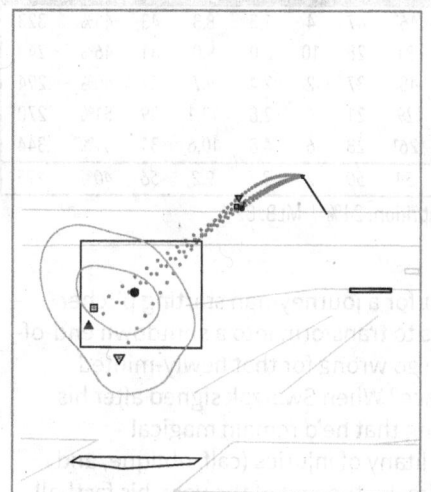

Pitch Shape vs RHH

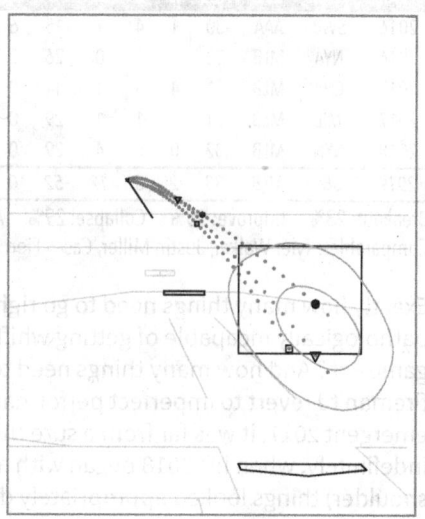

Type	Frequency	Velocity	H Movement	V Movement
● Fastball	54.9%	95.7 [110]	-3.4 [115]	-14.2 [105]
☐ Sinker	9.4%	94.5 [110]	-11.9 [106]	-19.2 [104]
+ Cutter				
▲ Changeup	12.1%	88.4 [112]	-12.1 [96]	-23 [113]
✕ Splitter				
▽ Slider	22.7%	83.4 [95]	8.8 [117]	-39.4 [81]
◇ Curveball	0.9%	79.5 [104]	10.9 [113]	-46.8 [103]
✦ Slow Curveball				
✱ Knuckleball				
▼ Screwball				

Anthony Swarzak RHP

Born: 09/10/85 Age: 33 Bats: R Throws: R
Height: 6'4" Weight: 215 Origin: Round 2, 2004 Draft (#61 overall)

YEAR	TEAM	LVL	AGE	W	L	SV	G	GS	IP	H	HR	BB/9	K/9	K	GB%	BABIP
2016	SWB	AAA	30	1	4	7	15	6	46.2	47	4	1.5	8.3	43	45%	.323
2016	NYA	MLB	30	1	2	0	26	0	31	28	10	2.0	9.0	31	46%	.240
2017	CHA	MLB	31	4	3	1	41	0	48.1	37	2	2.4	9.7	52	40%	.294
2017	MIL	MLB	31	2	1	1	29	0	29	21	4	2.8	12.1	39	51%	.270
2018	NYN	MLB	32	0	2	4	29	0	26.1	28	6	4.8	10.6	31	31%	.344
2019	SEA	MLB	33	2	3	12	52	0	54	50	7	3.7	9.2	56	40%	.295

Breakout: 23%   Improve: 35%   Collapse: 29%   Attrition: 21%   MLB: 82%
Comparables: Tyler Walker, Justin Miller, Casey Fien

Exactly how many things need to go right for a journeyman starting pitcher pathologically incapable of getting whiffs to transform into a shutdown end-of-game ace? And how many things need to go wrong for that newly-minted fireman to revert to imperfect performance? When Swarzak signed after his emergent 2017, it was far from a sure thing that he'd remain magical indefinitely; when his 2018 began with a litany of injuries (calf, oblique, and shoulder) things looked appropriately dire. By the end of the year, his fastball and slider were down a tick, his command went AWOL and he was salary ballast in a blockbuster trade instead of the reliever in demand. A change of scenery to the West Coast should give Swarzak the opportunity to remain in a late-game relief role, but it's more realistic to see him as a middle reliever. Not everything breaks right forever.

YEAR	TEAM	LVL	AGE	WHIP	ERA	DRA	WARP	MPH	FB%	WHF	CSP
2016	SWB	AAA	30	1.18	3.86	2.64	1.4				
2016	NYA	MLB	30	1.13	5.52	4.39	0.2	95.8	48.2	10.2	43.4
2017	CHA	MLB	31	1.03	2.23	2.92	1.2	95.9	48.8	15.5	47.3
2017	MIL	MLB	31	1.03	2.48	3.37	0.6	96.3	48.2	15.3	46.8
2018	NYN	MLB	32	1.59	6.15	5.71	-0.2	95.7	53.5	9.8	46.9
2019	SEA	MLB	33	1.32	4.24	4.47	0.4	94.9	49.3	12.9	45.5

Anthony Swarzak, continued

Pitch Shape vs LHH

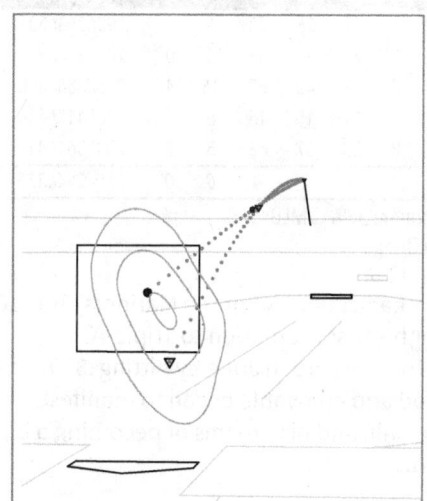

Pitch Shape vs RHH

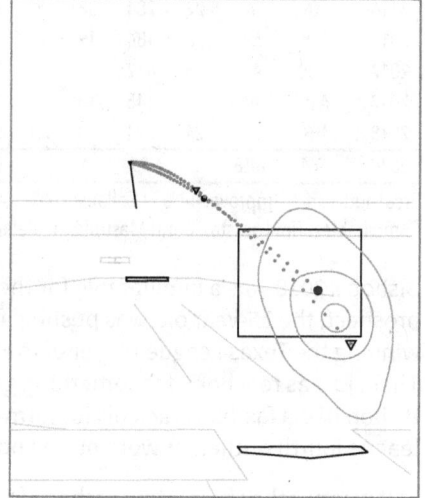

Type	Frequency	Velocity	H Movement	V Movement
● Fastball	53.5%	94.3 [106]	-6.1 [102]	-11.8 [112]
☐ Sinker				
+ Cutter				
▲ Changeup				
✕ Splitter				
▽ Slider	46.5%	85.7 [106]	3.9 [96]	-32.7 [101]
◇ Curveball				
✦ Slow Curveball				
✱ Knuckleball				
▼ Screwball				

Braden Bishop CF

Born: 08/22/93 Age: 25 Bats: R Throws: R
Height: 6'1" Weight: 190 Origin: Round 3, 2015 Draft (#94 overall)

YEAR	TEAM	LVL	AGE	PA	R	2B	3B	HR	RBI	BB	K	SB	CS	AVG/OBP/SLG
2016	CLN	A	22	284	38	5	1	1	21	25	48	6	1	.290/.363/.331
2016	BAK	A+	22	184	19	6	0	2	22	11	39	2	0	.247/.300/.319
2017	MOD	A+	23	412	71	25	3	2	32	45	65	16	4	.296/.385/.400
2017	ARK	AA	23	145	18	9	1	1	11	15	15	6	1	.336/.417/.448
2018	ARK	AA	24	394	70	20	0	8	33	37	68	5	2	.284/.361/.412
2019	SEA	MLB	25	35	4	1	0	1	4	2	8	0	0	.250/.294/.375

Breakout: 13% Improve: 44% Collapse: 0% Attrition: 38% MLB: 56%
Comparables: Tim Locastro, Darin Mastroianni, Rafael Ortega

Bishop's 2018 was a familiar tale for the organization. A (for the Mariners) Top-10 prospect, the 25-year old was pushing for his first promotion to Triple-A, winning the Texas League Player of the Month award in June by hitting .379. Then, just as real hope for something good and enjoyable began to manifest, Bishop had a fastball crack his forearm in half, and his dreams of becoming a big league fourth outfielder were put on hold.

It was another frustrating setback for the farm system, which has produced more tales of woe than big leaguers this decade. Bishop will most likely start next season back in the high minors, chasing fly balls and lost time in the cavernous center fields of Arkansas or Tacoma.

YEAR	TEAM	LVL	AGE	PA	DRC+	VORP	BABIP	BRR	FRAA	WARP
2016	CLN	A	22	284	124	13.8	.355	1.5	CF(40): -0.8, LF(14): -1.1	1.0
2016	BAK	A+	22	184	75	4.6	.310	-1.1	CF(34): -3.6, RF(7): -0.8	-0.9
2017	MOD	A+	23	412	124	23.2	.356	0.8	CF(70): -1.8, LF(14): 2.1	1.3
2017	ARK	AA	23	145	169	14.3	.373	-1.5	CF(31): 1.5	1.2
2018	ARK	AA	24	394	139	17.1	.331	-1.9	CF(81): -0.9, RF(2): -0.1	1.7
2019	SEA	MLB	25	35	74	0.3	.291	0.0	CF 0	0.0

Eric Filia RF

Born: 07/06/92 Age: 26 Bats: L Throws: R
Height: 6'0" Weight: 189 Origin: Round 20, 2016 Draft (#597 overall)

YEAR	TEAM	LVL	AGE	PA	R	2B	3B	HR	RBI	BB	K	SB	CS	AVG/OBP/SLG
2016	EVE	A-	23	292	43	19	1	4	46	39	19	10	5	.362/.450/.496
2017	MOD	A+	24	567	63	28	5	5	59	65	45	9	6	.326/.407/.434
2018	ARK	AA	25	345	44	14	1	2	38	44	30	1	0	.274/.371/.348
2019	*SEA*	*MLB*	*26*	*251*	*24*	*9*	*1*	*5*	*25*	*23*	*36*	*0*	*0*	*.233/.306/.343*

Breakout: 3% Improve: 22% Collapse: 1% Attrition: 15% MLB: 28%
Comparables: Cole Figueroa, Jermaine Curtis, Daniel Robertson

Filia is the answer to the question: What if we just make the entire player out of hit tool? With almost no draft or scout pedigree, the 2016 20th-round pick nonetheless spent his first two years in the low minors hitting like a Lumberjack Ichiro. After two years of running out of conversation topics with opposing first basemen, 2018 was poised to be Filia's opportunity to finally gain traction as a legitimate prospect.

Instead, what he earned was a 50-game suspension for a "drug of abuse" before the season started. Within weeks of returning to the field, he was traded to the Red Sox as a PTNBL. 2018, though, was not done tormenting Eric Filia. Like a reverse-Jesus, three days after being granted new life in a new system, he was returned to the Mariners as damaged goods, where his complete lack of power may have forever planted his prospect status in the tomb.

YEAR	TEAM	LVL	AGE	PA	DRC+	VORP	BABIP	BRR	FRAA	WARP
2016	EVE	A-	23	292	195	28.9	.376	0.6	RF(43): -2.2, CF(7): -0.3	1.7
2017	MOD	A+	24	567	152	39.7	.348	-0.6	RF(106): -11.7, 1B(12): -1.0	1.1
2018	ARK	AA	25	345	109	5.1	.297	-1.1	RF(44): -0.9, LF(11): -0.8	-0.2
2019	*SEA*	*MLB*	*26*	*251*	*82*	*0.9*	*.256*	*-0.4*	*RF -1, LF 0*	*0.0*

Jarred Kelenic CF

Born: 07/16/99 Age: 19 Bats: L Throws: L
Height: 6'1" Weight: 196 Origin: Round 1, 2018 Draft (#6 overall)

YEAR	TEAM	LVL	AGE	PA	R	2B	3B	HR	RBI	BB	K	SB	CS	AVG/OBP/SLG
2018	MTS	RK	18	51	9	2	2	1	9	4	11	4	0	.413/.451/.609
2018	KNG	RK	18	200	33	8	4	5	33	22	39	11	1	.253/.350/.431
2019	SEA	MLB	19	251	19	5	1	7	24	12	78	2	0	.133/.172/.254

Breakout: 5% Improve: 7% Collapse: 0% Attrition: 3% MLB: 9%
Comparables: Engel Beltre, Carlos Tocci, Franmil Reyes

Kelenic, the Mets' first-round selection in the 2018 draft, impressed in his pro debut, laying waste to the rookie leagues despite being a touch old for a prep prospect. Given the limited sample and unlimited hype, it's perhaps no surprise that opinions vary on the athletic outfielder: While the Baseball Prospectus in-house reports see him as a player with five average-or-better tools but perhaps without an elite carrying tool, other voices in the industry see superstar potential. The Mariners fall in the latter camp, targeting him as the prize return of the Robinson Cano blockbuster. They'll have to hope that the hit tool, power and approach all continue to develop in their system, because if they do Kelenic could grow into a well-rounded, dynamic outfield cornerstone.

YEAR	TEAM	LVL	AGE	PA	DRC+	VORP	BABIP	BRR	FRAA	WARP
2018	MTS	RK	18	51	184	8.0	.514	-0.1	CF(9): 2.0	0.5
2018	KNG	RK	18	200	124	15.2	.300	2.5	CF(43): 5.8	1.3
2019	SEA	MLB	19	251	8	-17.9	.156	0.4	CF 0	-1.9

Kyle Lewis CF

Born: 07/13/95 Age: 23 Bats: R Throws: R
Height: 6'4" Weight: 210 Origin: Round 1, 2016 Draft (#11 overall)

YEAR	TEAM	LVL	AGE	PA	R	2B	3B	HR	RBI	BB	K	SB	CS	AVG/OBP/SLG
2016	EVE	A-	20	135	26	8	5	3	26	16	22	3	0	.299/.385/.530
2017	MRN	RK	21	46	9	2	1	1	7	4	14	1	0	.263/.348/.447
2017	MOD	A+	21	167	20	4	0	6	24	15	38	2	1	.255/.323/.403
2018	MOD	A+	22	211	21	18	0	5	32	11	55	0	0	.260/.303/.429
2018	ARK	AA	22	152	18	8	0	4	20	17	32	1	0	.220/.309/.371
2019	SEA	MLB	23	251	22	7	1	8	28	15	70	0	0	.181/.230/.321

Breakout: 8% Improve: 14% Collapse: 1% Attrition: 7% MLB: 16%
Comparables: Bryan Petersen, Daniel Fields, Jake Cave

The good first: Two year removed from a catastrophic knee injury, Lewis appeared healthy in 2018. His future home on the field remains a corner outfield spot, but the knee allowed him to play nearly a full season without significant issue. Scouts indicate the tools that got him drafted 11th overall in 2016—athleticism, natural power and lift, as well as a rounded approach at the plate, remain. The tools and health combined as Lewis finished the year strong at Double-A Arkansas, hitting .253/.340/.470 over the final month of the season.

Now, the bad: Despite the fog of war that lingers over his performance because of his injuries, Lewis's tools have not yet translated to the performance worthy of a top prospect rating. The offense is going to have to improve significantly in order to justify a projection of anything but a part-time player on a below-average major league roster. While it's too early to make sweeping declarations, Lewis will be entering his age-24 season. It won't be too early much longer.

YEAR	TEAM	LVL	AGE	PA	DRC+	VORP	BABIP	BRR	FRAA	WARP
2016	EVE	A-	20	135	155	12.1	.344	-1.2	CF(27): -0.9	0.3
2017	MRN	RK	21	46	76	4.0	.360	1.4	CF(8): -1.0	-0.1
2017	MOD	A+	21	167	109	1.9	.299	-1.5	CF(13): 0.1	-0.1
2018	MOD	A+	22	211	104	8.9	.333	0.3	CF(23): -3.1, RF(11): -0.7	-0.3
2018	ARK	AA	22	152	90	0.2	.255	-2.0	CF(29): -2.6, RF(1): 0.0	-0.6
2019	SEA	MLB	23	251	46	-7.9	.217	-0.4	CF -1, RF 0	-1.0

Shed Long 2B

Born: 08/22/95   Age: 23   Bats: L   Throws: R
Height: 5'8"   Weight: 184   Origin: Round 12, 2013 Draft (#375 overall)

YEAR	TEAM	LVL	AGE	PA	R	2B	3B	HR	RBI	BB	K	SB	CS	AVG/OBP/SLG
2016	DYT	A	20	389	47	24	1	11	45	44	85	16	3	.281/.371/.457
2016	DAY	A+	20	159	22	6	4	4	30	10	35	5	1	.322/.371/.503
2017	DAY	A+	21	279	37	16	1	13	36	27	63	6	3	.312/.380/.543
2017	PEN	AA	21	160	13	6	2	3	14	19	31	3	1	.227/.319/.362
2018	PEN	AA	22	522	75	22	5	12	56	57	123	19	6	.261/.353/.412
2019	SEA	MLB	23	68	8	2	0	2	6	5	19	1	0	.194/.254/.323

Breakout: 12%   Improve: 26%   Collapse: 4%   Attrition: 16%   MLB: 36%
Comparables: Brandon Lowe, Carlos Asuaje, Dilson Herrera

A former 12th round pick, Long succeeded in his second crack at Double-A and could soon be manning the keystone at GABP. He's an adequate defender with enough speed to post double-digit steal totals, but it's his skill with the lumber that will determine his future. Long draws walks and has a quick bat that can pack a wallop, but his swing can get long at times and leads to rafts of strikeouts. If he maintains his patient approach and makes enough contact he could launch 15 bombs and be a top-of-the order spark plug; if not, there are still enough tools in this Shed to build a career on a big league bench.

YEAR	TEAM	LVL	AGE	PA	DRC+	VORP	BABIP	BRR	FRAA	WARP
2016	DYT	A	20	389	141	30.7	.346	3.2	2B(82): 2.0, 3B(3): -0.6	2.7
2016	DAY	A+	20	159	128	12.2	.393	1.3	2B(38): 3.0	1.0
2017	DAY	A+	21	279	147	21.5	.368	-1.1	2B(62): 5.4	1.9
2017	PEN	AA	21	160	103	1.9	.271	-2.4	2B(39): -1.7	-0.3
2018	PEN	AA	22	522	113	32.1	.333	3.7	2B(123): -1.9	1.4
2019	SEA	MLB	23	68	60	-0.7	.261	0.1	2B 0	-0.1

Cal Raleigh C

Born: 11/26/96   Age: 22   Bats: B   Throws: R
Height: 6'3"   Weight: 215   Origin: Round 3, 2018 Draft (#90 overall)

YEAR	TEAM	LVL	AGE	PA	R	2B	3B	HR	RBI	BB	K	SB	CS	AVG/OBP/SLG
2018	EVE	A-	21	167	25	10	1	8	29	18	29	1	1	.288/.367/.534
2019	SEA	MLB	22	251	22	8	0	10	30	14	68	0	0	.156/.200/.321

Breakout: 5%   Improve: 14%   Collapse: 0%   Attrition: 11%   MLB: 16%
Comparables: Blake Swihart, Austin Hedges, Christian Vazquez

If you're an offense-first catcher, you better provide some offense, and that's exactly what Raleigh did in his first season of professional ball. A third-round pick, the Florida State product presents a big silhouette behind the dish, and his pop times will require a lot of slide-stepping from whoever is pitching to him. Still, his receiving skills are solid to above-average and the possibility, even if small, that he can turn into a plus bat at catcher will keep him back there until he definitively proves he can't handle it. Given the Mariners organization-wide concerns at the position, Raleigh should advance quickly, provided that the bat leads.

YEAR	TEAM	LVL	AGE	PA	DRC+	VORP	BABIP	BRR	FRAA	WARP
2018	EVE	A-	21	167	140	11.6	.309	0.3	C(25): -0.2	0.7
2019	SEA	MLB	22	251	33	-10.1	.165	-0.5	C 0	-1.1

Julio Rodriguez RF

Born: 12/29/00 Age: 18 Bats: R Throws: R
Height: 6'3" Weight: 180 Origin: International Free Agent, 2017

YEAR	TEAM	LVL	AGE	PA	R	2B	3B	HR	RBI	BB	K	SB	CS	AVG/OBP/SLG
2018	DMR	RK	17	255	50	13	9	5	36	30	40	10	0	.315/.404/.525
2019	SEA	MLB	18	251	18	7	5	5	25	14	73	0	0	.174/.219/.313

Comparables: Adalberto Mondesi, Wilmer Flores, Tommy Brown

It's too early to get excited about Rodriguez, logically. Teenagers dominating other teenagers in the DSL is a world away from a star on the big league level. Trying to extrapolate something meaningful from the stats is a foolish, empty endeavor. Fortunately, there are professionals whose job it is to watch those same teenagers play baseball, and tell us which ones they think are going to be very, very good. We call them "scouts," and a good portion of them are very high on Rodriguez, to the point that he just may have the highest ceiling of any prospect in Seattle's farm. Of course even if he pans out perfectly he won't be a Mariner until practically the entire current big league roster is gone (or will get traded away for their sake), and there are far more ways a player this young can wash out than succeed, but if you have followed Seattle's farm system over the past 3-5 years you're readily acquainted with many of them. So, for 2019, Rodriguez will be a shiny beacon of hope and possibility. The Mariners and their fans can certainly use it.

YEAR	TEAM	LVL	AGE	PA	DRC+	VORP	BABIP	BRR	FRAA	WARP
2018	DMR	RK	17	255	165	33.9	.364	0.6	RF(45): 8.1, CF(6): -0.1	2.5
2019	SEA	MLB	18	251	38	-11.0	.223	0.6	RF 2, CF 0	-1.0

Ichiro Suzuki   RF

Born: 10/22/73   Age: 45   Bats: L   Throws: R
Height: 5'11"   Weight: 175   Origin: International Free Agent, 2000

YEAR	TEAM	LVL	AGE	PA	R	2B	3B	HR	RBI	BB	K	SB	CS	AVG/OBP/SLG
2016	MIA	MLB	42	365	48	15	5	1	22	30	42	10	2	.291/.354/.376
2017	MIA	MLB	43	215	19	6	0	3	20	17	35	1	1	.255/.318/.332
2018	SEA	MLB	44	47	5	0	0	0	0	3	7	0	0	.205/.255/.205
2019	SEA	MLB	45	251	29	10	1	3	21	21	44	4	1	.261/.328/.361

Breakout: 0%   Improve: 0%   Collapse: 23%   Attrition: 5%   MLB: 57%
Comparables: Omar Vizquel, Sam Rice, Pete Rose

What then to make of this man; this slap-hitting, fence-climbing, quote-generating world conqueror? His in-game achievements—the infield single, the broken bat looper parachuted over the third baseman's head, the stolen base—are, by design, performed in second, and at incredible speed. By contrast his career accomplishments have taken a full lifetime to accumulate.

This comment should serve as an attempt to summarize that lifetime. It should flail and sputter as it somehow attempts to describe one our sport's truly unique athletes, and men. It should try to put a bow on the records, the pressure his game put on a defense, his ability to dominate the sport without hitting a ball out of the infield. It would fail to do all that, but it should try.

It will not try, however, because Ichiro will not let it. He is 45 years old, and will not stop playing baseball. In 2018 he exercised every bit of the cache his legendary career allowed him, and, after a few months of replacement-level play for the Mariners, built his own job title and duties out of thin air. At every turn he, and anyone associated with Seattle, pointed out that he "is not retired".

The Mariners open the 2019 season in Ichiro's native Japan. He will play, at least a bit, and the duty of writing his career's summary in these pages will pass to next year's annual. This is good because, like the man himself, it is impossible.

YEAR	TEAM	LVL	AGE	PA	DRC+	VORP	BABIP	BRR	FRAA	WARP
2016	MIA	MLB	42	365	91	8.5	.329	-1.7	RF(54): -1.9, LF(14): 2.9	0.3
2017	MIA	MLB	43	215	78	-3.0	.297	-2.7	RF(16): -0.1, CF(10): -1.3	-0.1
2018	SEA	MLB	44	47	77	-2.6	.243	0.9	LF(11): -0.2, RF(1): 0.1	0.0
2019	SEA	MLB	45	251	85	1.5	.308	-1.1	LF 1, RF 0	0.3

Evan White 1B

Born: 04/26/96 Age: 23 Bats: R Throws: L
Height: 6'3" Weight: 205 Origin: Round 1, 2017 Draft (#17 overall)

YEAR	TEAM	LVL	AGE	PA	R	2B	3B	HR	RBI	BB	K	SB	CS	AVG/OBP/SLG
2017	EVE	A-	21	55	6	1	1	3	12	6	6	1	1	.277/.345/.532
2018	MOD	A+	22	538	72	27	7	11	66	52	103	4	3	.303/.375/.458
2019	SEA	MLB	23	251	24	7	1	7	29	17	62	0	0	.222/.276/.360

Breakout: 6% Improve: 15% Collapse: 0% Attrition: 8% MLB: 17%
Comparables: Shane Peterson, Ronald Guzman, David Cooper

The Mariners farm system has long been a trash-filled, post-apocalyptic wasteland, but White may just be the plant from WALL-E, poking his head above the rubble, telling us it's safe to return. A superb athlete for a first baseman, White lowered his hands to generate a better swing plane. The result was a very encouraging power explosion in August. White slugged over .700 in the season's final month, while continuing to show promising contact and on-base skills. It's still a little weird that the M's haven't at least tried out his athleticism at a corner outfield spot, but this new version of his bat might hold up even at first.

For a 22-year-old, first-round draft pick, destroying High-A pitching doesn't put White exceptionally far ahead on the development curve, though he built upon the performance in the Arizona Fall League. However, it also doesn't put him woefully, distressingly behind, and for the Mariners, that's an accomplishment in and of itself.

YEAR	TEAM	LVL	AGE	PA	DRC+	VORP	BABIP	BRR	FRAA	WARP
2017	EVE	A-	21	55	124	3.7	.250	-0.1	1B(8): -0.6	-0.1
2018	MOD	A+	22	538	144	38.3	.363	-0.5	1B(106): 5.5	2.1
2019	SEA	MLB	23	251	68	-5.1	.268	-0.1	1B 1	-0.4

Sam Carlson   RHP

Born: 12/03/98   Age: 20   Bats: R   Throws: R
Height: 6'4"   Weight: 195   Origin: Round 2, 2017 Draft (#55 overall)

YEAR	TEAM	LVL	AGE	W	L	SV	G	GS	IP	H	HR	BB/9	K/9	K	GB%	BABIP
2019	SEA	MLB	20	2	3	0	7	7	32	31	4	4.8	7.0	25	53%	.274

Comparables: Deolis Guerra, Alex Burnett, Mauricio Cabrera

For someone a year from being old enough to legally drink, Carlson is awfully young to feel so behind. After spending high school pitching in the brief Minnesota spring, Seattle's second-round pick from 2017 threw three innings in the AZL before being shut down with elbow discomfort. When an offseason of rest did not provide healing, further investigation revealed a torn UCL. Tommy John surgery last July means Carlson may not pitch until 2020. He may be able to order that beer before he steps on a mound again.

YEAR	TEAM	LVL	AGE	WHIP	ERA	DRA	WARP	MPH	FB%	WHF	CSP
2019	SEA	MLB	20	1.50	5.70	6.11	-0.2				

Justin Dunn RHP

Born: 09/22/95 Age: 23 Bats: R Throws: R
Height: 6'2" Weight: 185 Origin: Round 1, 2016 Draft (#19 overall)

YEAR	TEAM	LVL	AGE	W	L	SV	G	GS	IP	H	HR	BB/9	K/9	K	GB%	BABIP
2016	BRO	A-	20	1	1	0	11	8	30	25	1	3.0	10.5	35	46%	.320
2017	SLU	A+	21	5	6	0	20	16	95^1	101	5	4.5	7.1	75	44%	.322
2018	SLU	A+	22	2	3	0	9	9	45^2	43	2	3.0	10.1	51	42%	.325
2018	BIN	AA	22	6	5	0	15	15	89^2	85	7	3.7	10.5	105	47%	.345
2019	SEA	MLB	23	6	7	0	21	21	105^1	102	13	4.3	9.0	106	40%	.305

Breakout: 8% Improve: 15% Collapse: 5% Attrition: 15% MLB: 24%
Comparables: Glen Perkins, D.J. Mitchell, Cody Reed

An uninspiring full-season debut in 2017 led more than a few to prematurely apply the "bust" tag to this former first-round pick out of Boston College, but last season saw Dunn turn around some of the naysayers. He still has trouble with consistency—whether it's keeping his velocity steady, retaining his control or smoothing performance from start to start—but his fastball-slider combo is good enough to make him either a bullpen weapon if nothing changes or a no. 3 starter if a third pitch ever comes along. It will now be on the Mariners to finish off his development and see if there's any chance he might one day replace the now-departed James Paxton or Edwin Diaz.

YEAR	TEAM	LVL	AGE	WHIP	ERA	DRA	WARP	MPH	FB%	WHF	CSP
2016	BRO	A-	20	1.17	1.50	2.19	1.1				
2017	SLU	A+	21	1.56	5.00	4.27	1.0				
2018	SLU	A+	22	1.27	2.36	3.43	1.0				
2018	BIN	AA	22	1.36	4.22	3.48	1.9				
2019	SEA	MLB	23	1.44	4.60	4.92	0.7				

Matt Festa RHP

Born: 03/11/93 Age: 26 Bats: R Throws: R
Height: 6'2" Weight: 195 Origin: Round 7, 2016 Draft (#207 overall)

YEAR	TEAM	LVL	AGE	W	L	SV	G	GS	IP	H	HR	BB/9	K/9	K	GB%	BABIP
2016	EVE	A-	23	6	2	0	14	8	60^1	60	3	2.1	8.7	58	49%	.324
2017	MOD	A+	24	4	2	6	42	1	69^2	61	7	2.5	12.8	99	44%	.327
2018	ARK	AA	25	5	2	20	44	0	49	50	6	2.2	12.3	67	47%	.364
2018	SEA	MLB	25	0	0	0	8	1	8^1	13	0	2.2	4.3	4	33%	.394
2019	SEA	MLB	26	2	2	0	33	2	34^2	34	5	3.4	9.4	36	41%	.300

Breakout: 13%   Improve: 21%   Collapse: 8%   Attrition: 18%   MLB: 33%
Comparables: Evan Scribner, Cody Ege, Jonathan Aro

Life itself is a resplendent, kaleidoscopic, orgy of variety. Here we see one of its rarest, and most exotic strains: The Jerry Dipoto Draft Pick in the Major Leagues. Although typically found in abundance in the mid-minors, where they serve largely as a sort of feudal working class for their larger and more gifted brethren, there is a micro-species that breaks free from the ball fields of Appalachia and plains of Texas and migrates to the big leagues. Festa represents the first sighting of this evolutionary oddity in Seattle. While his fastball-slider combination aren't at the elite level, his polish and command should make him a viable bullpen contributor, and an enduring testament to the evolutionary power of our species. Velocity finds a way.

YEAR	TEAM	LVL	AGE	WHIP	ERA	DRA	WARP	MPH	FB%	WHF	CSP
2016	EVE	A-	23	1.23	3.73	3.10	1.4				
2017	MOD	A+	24	1.15	3.23	2.55	1.9				
2018	ARK	AA	25	1.27	2.76	2.58	1.4				
2018	SEA	MLB	25	1.80	2.16	7.26	-0.2	94.0	47.8	7.5	51.2
2019	SEA	MLB	26	1.35	4.49	4.70	0.2	93.6	48.7	7.7	52.1

Seattle Mariners 2019

Logan Gilbert   RHP

Born: 05/05/97   Age: 22   Bats: R   Throws: R
Height: 6'6"   Weight: 225   Origin: Round 1, 2018 Draft (#14 overall)

From the same college that brought you smash hits Corey Kluber and Jacob deGrom, Seattle is betting they have another winner on their hands with the 6'6" Gilbert, drafting him 14th overall in last year's draft. The right-hander saw his stock dip along with his velocity in midseason, only to see both return by draft time. It's that fastball, which reportedly averaged 94-97 MPH in the Cape Cod League, along with his large frame and athleticism, that rounds out the profile of a quality mid-rotation starter. Even though a long college season and mid-summer illness kept him from throwing even one professional inning in 2018, he is arguably already Seattle's top pitching prospect, and a player theoretically primed to move quickly should all go according to plan.

Yusei Kikuchi LHP

Born: 06/17/91 Age: 28 Bats: L Throws: L
Height: 6'0" Weight: 194 Origin: International Free Agent, 2018

YEAR	TEAM	LVL	AGE	W	L	SV	G	GS	IP	H	HR	BB/9	K/9	K	GB%	BABIP
2019	SEA	MLB	28	8	10	0	26	26	148	140	19	3.1	8.4	139	46%	.293

Breakout: 25% Improve: 59% Collapse: 20% Attrition: 4% MLB: 93%
Comparables: Patrick Corbin, Mat Latos, Jordan Zimmermann

This could have been Kikuchi's ninth entry in the BP Annual: In 2009, he considered becoming the first major Japanese high school prospect to circumnavigate the NPB and sign with an MLB team. He opted not to, and instead enjoyed a successful career with the Seibu Lions, making three All-Star games and throwing the league's hardest fastball, sitting in the low-to-mid nineties. He pairs it with an excellent hard slider, as well as a changeup and slow curve that technically exist. Scouts generally agree that Kikuchi looks like a solid number two starter, which makes him Seattle's clear number one starter, which means that his first major league start will ironically be in Japan against the Athletics. The main concern, and the price he paid for his national loyalty, is an overworked shoulder that diminished his 2018 season, though he appeared to finish the year healthy. The Mariners are likely to be more cautious with their newest star, especially given the level of stakes they're likely to offer him the next couple of years.

YEAR	TEAM	LVL	AGE	WHIP	ERA	DRA	WARP	MPH	FB%	WHF	CSP
2019	SEA	MLB	28	1.29	4.23	4.53	1.5				

Wyatt Mills RHP

Born: 01/25/95 Age: 24 Bats: R Throws: R
Height: 6'3" Weight: 175 Origin: Round 3, 2017 Draft (#93 overall)

YEAR	TEAM	LVL	AGE	W	L	SV	G	GS	IP	H	HR	BB/9	K/9	K	GB%	BABIP
2017	EVE	A-	22	0	1	2	7	0	7	3	0	3.9	14.1	11	50%	.214
2017	CLN	A	22	0	1	4	11	0	13^1	5	0	4.1	12.1	18	57%	.179
2018	MOD	A+	23	6	0	11	35	0	42^1	29	1	1.9	10.4	49	54%	.277
2018	ARK	AA	23	0	2	0	9	0	10^2	18	0	3.4	8.4	10	42%	.450
2019	SEA	MLB	24	2	1	2	36	0	38^2	35	5	4.3	9.3	40	45%	.295

Breakout: 0% Improve: 0% Collapse: 1% Attrition: 1% MLB: 1%
Comparables: Colton Murray, Adam Kolarek, Branden Pinder

There are a lot of words in the English language for the act of throwing a baseball: toss, heave, fling, whip, fire, lob, sidearm, underhand, flip, and on. What Mills does is, in the opinion of these pages, best described as "slanging." His near-sidearm delivery results in good arm side run, which when coupled with 92-94 mph velocity, project him as a tough at-bat for right-handers. While he struggled in his short stint in Double-A last year, look for Mills to start there in 2019. If he stays on track the stuff and record appears to have him ticketed for a major league bullpen no later than 2020.

YEAR	TEAM	LVL	AGE	WHIP	ERA	DRA	WARP	MPH	FB%	WHF	CSP
2017	EVE	A-	22	0.86	2.57	3.01	0.2				
2017	CLN	A	22	0.82	1.35	4.14	0.1				
2018	MOD	A+	23	0.90	1.91	3.59	0.7				
2018	ARK	AA	23	2.06	10.12	3.98	0.1				
2019	SEA	MLB	24	1.38	4.49	4.80	0.1				

Justus Sheffield LHP

Born: 05/13/96 Age: 23 Bats: L Throws: L
Height: 6'0" Weight: 200 Origin: Round 1, 2014 Draft (#31 overall)

YEAR	TEAM	LVL	AGE	W	L	SV	G	GS	IP	H	HR	BB/9	K/9	K	GB%	BABIP
2016	LYN	A+	20	7	5	0	19	19	95^1	91	6	3.8	8.8	93	45%	.321
2016	TAM	A+	20	3	1	0	5	5	26	14	0	3.5	9.3	27	45%	.226
2017	TRN	AA	21	7	6	0	17	17	93^1	94	14	3.2	7.9	82	48%	.293
2018	TRN	AA	22	1	2	0	5	5	28	16	1	4.5	12.5	39	44%	.259
2018	SWB	AAA	22	6	4	0	20	15	88	66	3	3.7	8.6	84	46%	.264
2018	NYA	MLB	22	0	0	0	3	0	2^2	4	1	10.1	0.0	0	55%	.300
2019	SEA	MLB	23	4	5	0	13	13	74	67	10	4.1	9.4	77	43%	.292

Breakout: 21% Improve: 26% Collapse: 14% Attrition: 33% MLB: 48%
Comparables: Michael Fulmer, Matt Magill, Giovanni Soto

There's nothing quite like the post-trade prospect re-evaluation. Ranked as the 57th best prospect according to BP last year, Sheffield built upon past success, albeit unsteadily, culminating in his brief, nerve-wracking major league debut, where he said his "legs felt like Jell-O." He appeared to be a brisk, contract-extending April tune-up away from a rotation spot when he was shipped to Seattle as the headliner in the James Paxton trade. Suddenly there were all sorts of concerns about his makeup, his command, and the floor of "talented but inconsistent relief arm" flew up at him. He'll get a chance to prove his worth in Seattle, after the usual six-week period of reflection, during which time he switches from "good prospect in overcrowded system" to Seattle's obvious No. 1. The key will be his ability to find the strike zone, and the Mariners obviously feel that they, unlike the organization that produces an elite arm every three weeks, can unlock the secrets to control the zone.

YEAR	TEAM	LVL	AGE	WHIP	ERA	DRA	WARP	MPH	FB%	WHF	CSP
2016	LYN	A+	20	1.37	3.59	3.57	2.1				
2016	TAM	A+	20	0.92	1.73	2.95	0.7				
2017	TRN	AA	21	1.36	3.18	3.54	1.8				
2018	TRN	AA	22	1.07	2.25	3.47	0.6				
2018	SWB	AAA	22	1.16	2.56	4.27	1.2				
2018	NYA	MLB	22	2.62	10.12	6.56	-0.1	95.7	54.4	1.8	38.3
2019	SEA	MLB	23	1.36	4.38	4.70	0.6	95.6	56.3	1.8	39.7

Erik Swanson RHP

Born: 09/04/93 Age: 25 Bats: R Throws: R
Height: 6'3" Weight: 235 Origin: Round 8, 2014 Draft (#246 overall)

YEAR	TEAM	LVL	AGE	W	L	SV	G	GS	IP	H	HR	BB/9	K/9	K	GB%	BABIP
2016	HIC	A	22	6	4	1	19	15	81^1	77	4	2.8	8.6	78	53%	.319
2016	CSC	A	22	0	1	0	5	2	15	14	0	3.0	9.0	15	50%	.333
2017	TAM	A+	23	7	3	0	20	20	100^1	115	10	1.3	7.5	84	42%	.344
2018	TRN	AA	24	5	0	0	8	7	42^2	22	0	3.2	11.6	55	36%	.253
2018	SWB	AAA	24	3	2	0	14	13	72^1	63	10	1.7	9.7	78	37%	.283
2019	SEA	MLB	25	3	4	0	10	10	50	50	8	3.0	8.6	48	40%	.295

Breakout: 11% Improve: 19% Collapse: 13% Attrition: 26% MLB: 36%
Comparables: Sean Gilmartin, Jeremy Hefner, Cory Luebke

Swanson likely wouldn't have warranted much discussion in any other year, but that changes when you're part of a trade for James Paxton alongside Justus Sheffield. While Sheffield may be the headliner, Swanson compared favorably from a statistical standpoint, actually outperforming the top prospect between Double- and Triple-A by DRA. That fun fact will probably get employed more as an indictment on the former than credit to the latter, who looks every bit the part of a stodgy fourth or fifth starter. While he was blocked by what is now a stocked rotation, Swanson now gets the chance to put that performance to the test at the big leagues, on a rebuilding ball club that will give him a leash to sink or swim. If his fastball is for real, as Jerry Dipoto likely believes, then Seattle's front office may have smuggled a full-time starter behind a possibly more risky high-upside headliner.

YEAR	TEAM	LVL	AGE	WHIP	ERA	DRA	WARP	MPH	FB%	WHF	CSP
2016	HIC	A	22	1.25	3.43	3.26	1.7				
2016	CSC	A	22	1.27	3.60	2.65	0.4				
2017	TAM	A+	23	1.29	3.95	4.34	1.1				
2018	TRN	AA	24	0.87	0.42	3.54	0.9				
2018	SWB	AAA	24	1.06	3.86	3.55	1.6				
2019	SEA	MLB	25	1.33	4.62	4.97	0.3				

LINEOUTS

Hitters

HITTER	POS	TEAM	LVL	AGE	PA	R	2B	3B	HR	RBI	BB	K	SB	CS	AVG/OBP/SLG	DRC+	WARP
Joey Curletta	1B	ARK	AA	24	556	70	24	0	23	94	81	130	1	1	.282/.383/.482	153	1.5
David Freitas	C	TAC	AAA	29	167	15	12	1	4	23	17	27	0	0	.349/.428/.527	147	1.4
	C	SEA	MLB	29	106	9	6	0	1	5	8	25	0	0	.215/.277/.312	74	0.2
Cesar Izturis	SS	MRN	Rk	18	206	28	7	0	1	12	12	44	5	3	.245/.304/.298	75	-0.5
Luis Liberato	LF	MOD	A+	22	370	48	20	2	11	44	34	63	2	5	.250/.317/.424	112	0.9
Jose Lobaton	C	LVG	AAA	33	151	22	9	0	8	27	18	31	1	0	.348/.430/.598	159	1.5
	C	NYN	MLB	33	57	3	2	1	0	4	7	15	0	0	.143/.246/.224	66	0.0
Ian Miller	CF	TAC	AAA	26	478	60	16	3	2	41	43	89	33	9	.261/.333/.327	74	-0.4
Kris Negron	3B	ARI	MLB	32	3	0	0	0	0	1	0	0	0	0	.333/.333/.333	76	0.0
	3B	RNO	AAA	32	425	71	17	5	15	45	43	121	10	3	.283/.368/.477	107	2.2
	3B	SEA	MLB	32	30	6	0	0	1	3	1	9	2	0	.207/.233/.310	78	0.1
Juan Querecuto	SS	DMR	Rk	17	280	37	8	2	3	29	25	54	3	6	.243/.331/.329	103	0.6
Joe Rizzo	3B	MOD	A+	20	508	46	21	2	4	55	40	108	6	1	.241/.303/.321	77	-1.0
Dom Thompson-Williams	OF	CSC	A	23	40	7	1	0	5	9	2	7	3	2	.378/.425/.811	171	0.2
	OF	TAM	A+	23	375	56	16	4	17	65	31	95	17	7	.290/.356/.517	126	0.9
Donnie Walton	2B	MOD	A+	24	256	35	12	3	3	19	30	37	8	3	.309/.402/.433	149	1.1
	2B	ARK	AA	24	238	22	14	1	1	22	21	34	3	1	.236/.325/.327	84	0.2
Nick Zammarelli	RF	MOD	A+	23	508	60	30	6	10	60	39	136	5	1	.274/.336/.431	114	-1.7

Joey Curletta sounds like a name you would give to a bodybuilder NPC in a bad JRPG, but if the organization's Minor League Hitter of the Year can continue to control the zone, he may graduate to playable DLC. ⓧ **David Freitas** has kind eyes, soft hands, and unfortunately for his baseball career, a softer bat. It is recommended he look into a low-emissions, high-MPG automobile for that Tacoma-Seattle commute. ⓧ By 2100, if our earth remains, all baseball players will be the offspring of former big leaguers. Mack Trout will be the game's best player, Krys Sale its most dominating pitcher, and Cesar Izturis V, **Cesar Izturis Jr**'s great-grandson, will hit .240 in AA while playing slightly above-average defense at shortstop. ⓧ Repeating High-A, **Luis Liberato's** offensive 2018 was a near carbon copy of his previous year. The ability to punish mistakes is a good starting point, but he'll need to start occasionally being good against opponents who are also being good. ⓧ It's a minor miracle that **Jose Lobaton** snuck into 22 games last year, but he's quite the advertisement for the career security that comes with being a warm body who can wear a chest protector. ⓧ **Ian Miller** has a negative scouting report as his headline image on Twitter, presumably to serve as inspiration to beat the haters. The report is worth reading, as it's largely very accurate. ⓧ The Mariners largely wasted a roster spot on Andrew Romine in

2018, which makes the idea of **Kris Negron** so appealing moving forward. He has a very nice mustache, you see. ⚾ *You swung so fast at that hanger / Only eighteen but just hit a banger / And it goes back, back, back, to the trees / Didn't you,* **Juan Querecuto**? ⚾ Any prospect shine has almost completely worn off **Joe Rizzo**. At only twenty-one there's still plenty of time for the former 2nd-round pick, but he'll need to start showing he can slug higher than the mid-.300's if he wants to find himself on organizational top-10 lists, and/or move into the mid-minors. ⚾ The Dipoto Collective loves nothing more than a swing adjustment, and none were bigger than that of **Dom Thompson-Williams**, who put it together at age 23 in Low and High-A ball. The toolsy former Yankee product makes lots of easy outs, but a high HR/FB rate and low infield fly rate suggests he might be onto something. ⚾ How to make **Donnie Walton** at home: Start with two quarts of Bloomquist stock, simmering at 200 degrees. Add two cups chopped Ryan Theriot, a peel of Brooks Conrad, and two-thirds cup of melted Kelby Tomlinson. Stir until fully mixed, add powdered David Eckstein to flavor. Serve, and enjoy. ⚾ Every baseball player needs a standout tool to get noticed. Joey Gallo had power. Billy Hamilton had speed. In **Nick Zammarelli's** case his, uh, well, his name is very fun to say loudly and dramatically.

Pitchers

PITCHER	TEAM	LVL	AGE	W	L	SV	G	GS	IP	H	HR	BB/9	K/9	K	GB%	WHIP	ERA	DRA	WARP
Shawn Armstrong	TAC	AAA	27	2	5	15	49	0	56	38	3	4.2	13.2	82	35%	1.14	1.77	2.16	1.9
	SEA	MLB	27	0	1	1	14	0	14^2	9	1	1.8	9.2	15	44%	0.82	1.23	4.40	0.1
Gerson Bautista	BIN	AA	23	1	0	0	6	0	9^1	12	0	0.0	14.5	15	42%	1.29	4.82	1.88	0.3
	NYN	MLB	23	0	1	0	5	0	4^1	8	2	10.4	6.2	3	35%	3.00	12.46	7.18	-0.1
	LVG	AAA	23	3	1	3	31	0	39^2	54	3	4.1	12.3	54	24%	1.82	5.22	4.74	0.2
Chasen Bradford	TAC	AAA	28	0	0	1	7	0	6^2	5	0	0.0	5.4	4	48%	0.75	0.00	3.69	0.1
	SEA	MLB	28	5	0	0	46	0	53^2	55	9	2.3	6.4	38	46%	1.29	3.69	5.46	-0.3
Nabil Crismatt	LVG	AAA	23	3	4	0	9	9	38^2	61	8	4.4	8.1	35	48%	2.07	8.84	4.67	0.4
	BIN	AA	23	8	6	0	18	18	105^1	95	8	3.2	9.0	105	47%	1.25	3.59	3.70	2.0
Roenis Elias	PAW	AAA	29	1	0	1	4	0	7^1	2	1	2.5	11.0	9	47%	0.55	1.23	2.61	0.2
	TAC	AAA	29	2	4	0	10	7	33^2	32	1	4.0	8.3	31	44%	1.40	4.54	4.30	0.4
	SEA	MLB	29	3	1	0	23	4	51	46	1	2.8	6.0	34	35%	1.22	2.65	5.35	-0.2
Cory Gearrin	SFN	MLB	32	1	1	1	35	0	30	33	5	3.9	9.3	31	34%	1.53	4.20	4.57	0.1
	TEX	MLB	32	1	0	0	21	0	21^1	13	2	2.5	8.4	20	52%	0.89	2.53	4.97	0.0
	OAK	MLB	32	0	0	0	6	0	6	10	0	3.0	3.0	2	50%	2.00	6.00	3.91	0.1
Joey Gerber	EVE	A-	21	1	0	6	13	0	14	9	0	3.9	13.5	21	59%	1.07	1.93	2.71	0.4
	CLN	A	21	0	0	2	9	0	11^2	9	0	3.9	17.0	22	35%	1.20	2.31	2.00	0.4
Max Povse	TAC	AAA	24	1	6	0	8	8	36^2	40	6	6.9	11.0	45	43%	1.85	8.84	4.52	0.4
	ARK	AA	24	4	3	0	10	10	60^2	62	2	2.8	8.9	60	47%	1.34	3.41	4.20	0.8
Zac Rosscup	LAN	MLB	30	0	1	0	17	0	11^1	9	3	3.2	15.9	20	30%	1.15	4.76	3.75	0.2
Nick Rumbelow	TAC	AAA	26	1	0	2	13	0	17^2	13	1	4.1	12.7	25	38%	1.19	2.04	2.76	0.5
	SEA	MLB	26	0	0	0	13	0	17^2	19	6	3.1	8.2	16	33%	1.42	6.11	5.95	-0.2
Ricardo Sanchez	DNV	Rk	21	1	0	0	2	2	11^2	11	1	2.3	6.9	9	54%	1.20	3.09	3.72	0.3
	MIS	AA	21	2	5	0	13	13	57^2	65	3	3.7	6.9	44	41%	1.54	4.06	6.19	-0.6
Sam Tuivailala	SLN	MLB	25	3	3	0	31	0	31^2	35	3	3.1	7.4	26	50%	1.45	3.69	4.77	0.1
	SEA	MLB	25	1	0	0	5	0	5^1	6	0	1.7	6.8	4	56%	1.31	1.69	2.93	0.1
Art Warren	ARK	AA	25	1	2	2	14	0	15^2	10	0	8.0	12.6	22	39%	1.53	1.72	3.37	0.3

It is tempting to ridicule **Shawn Armstrong** for letting nominative determinisim direct his vocational pursuits. But as long as he can keep that walk rate down, the Mariners won't have to worry about his low-90s fastball making him liable in a suit for false advertising. ⓧ Relief prospect **Gerson Bautista** was able to top 101 miles per hour during one of his extremely brief and ineffective stints with the Mets last year. Because said fastball is arrow-straight, this is likely the last time "Gerson Bautista" and "top 101" will ever be found in the same sentence. ⓧ From June 17th until August 31st, the Mariners went 1-13 in games **Chasen Bradford** appeared in. This is probably an indication that he's simply a mop-up reliever, but we should at least consider the possibility that he's the human equivalent of a mummy's curse. ⓧ **Nabil Crismatt** has an extremely *Star Wars* name but an earthbound prospect profile. His late start has him aging out of prospect status and his ceiling is more Stormtrooper than Skywalker. ⓧ It may not be as catchy, but "Life is like a **Roenis Elias** Curveball: Slow, loopy, and prone to massive failure" is much more authentic to the human condition. ⓧ In the Kevin Smith movie *Dogma*, Jay, Silent Bob and Linda Fiorentino's Bethany are motoring down a dark highway at 95 mph with Jay at the wheel. Bethany shouts over the noise of the engine and the music, "What gear are you in?" Jay responds, bewildered, "Geeearrr??" Cut to the three peering into the smoking engine. This is a Lineout, so we have to say a name now: **Cory Gearrin**. ⓧ **Joey Gerber** struck out a ridiculous number of batters—over 40 percent—in his abbreviated introduction to pro ball. A late bloomer in college, he's a relief prospect only, but on the bright side, Mariners fans: He's a prospect. ⓧ The term for a player who succeeds in AAA but struggles in MLB is "AAAA player". **Max Povse**, however, succeeds in AA but struggles in AAA. Scholars are split on whether this makes him a "AA.5" or "AAa" player. ⓧ **Zac Rosscup** tossed an immaculate inning in late August against the Mariners, making him one of only 87 pitchers to ever achieve such a feat. So that's cool. ⓧ Jerry Dipoto asked the Yankees for **Nick Rumbelow** on purpose, meaning that he knew his name, and didn't have to awkwardly google how to spell it. This is high praise for both men. Excellent work, gents. ⓧ The Braves were high enough on **Ricardo Sanchez** to protect him from the Rule 5 draft, but their reward was a mediocre season at Double-A and more health concerns. ⓧ Every Mariners season, no matter how promising or postseason-destined it may appear, is doomed to end in misery and pain. Still, losing **Sam Tuivailala** to a snapped Achilles in August seemed a little too on the nose, even for whichever hamfisted hack Fate employs to write out the script for the cursed franchise. ⓧ In EMPIRE RECORDS (1995), young record store employee Lucas responds to an inquiry as to his purpose behind gluing quarters to the floor with, "I don't feel I need to explain my art to you, Warren." This serves as good an explanation for **Art Warren's** 2018 walk rate as we can conceive. ⓧ **Rob Whalen** is a strong arm from the right, and despite the incredible advantage society gives someone from that position, he's floundered in large part due to his own failures.

Mariners Prospects

The State of the System:
"Finally there is clarity and there is purpose after all, but every night ends the same as I'm collapsing once more by your side." – Death Cab for Cutie, "Debate Exposes Doubt"

The Top Ten:

1   **Justus Sheffield**   **LHP**   OFP: 60   Likely: 50   ETA: Debuted in 2018
Born: 05/13/96   Age: 23   Bats: L   Throws: L   Height: 6'0"   Weight: 200
Origin: Round 1, 2014 Draft (#31 overall)

The Report: We talk a lot about the concept of "prospect fatigue." Sometimes you've seen a guy for years and years and he's fine. He's exactly what you expected him to be at this point in the timeline, no more and no less. You've probably written about him a dozen times over the past few years. He might've been part of a major transaction or two. He was probably a high pick or expensive IFA. And you just get sort of tired of talking about him, so the report comes across lower than it should. Really, there's absolutely nothing wrong.

You're probably not supposed to admit this as a prospect writer, but I do try to be transparent, and Justus Sheffield is the epitome of prospect fatigue for me. Sheffield has been a big name prospect since he was in high school. He has a brother with a similar profile. He's exactly where he "should" be right now. He's ranked at the same basic spot on all of our lists for years. He's got the same grades, the same strengths, the same weaknesses. He's been traded twice, as a primary piece in a major deadline trade and a major winter trade, so we've talked about him a lot in several different evaluative contexts. It feels like I've written a million different Justus Sheffield reports, and it feels like the well is dry on new ways to spin him.

But, hey, this is his first time on Seattle's list, right? So here goes… Sheffield is a fastball/slider/change lefty who debuted in a September relief cameo for the Yankees. He was 94-96 MPH with the fastball then, although he's frequently sat a tick or two little lower as a starter and has also occasionally touched a tick or two higher. The slider is most often a tight mid-80s offering, and it's close to if not already a present plus pitch. He'll also sometimes manipulate it down to a slurve that sometimes gets labeled a curveball, and it is the out pitch he relies on most at present. His changeup flashes plus with a bit less consistency, but it's hard and dives.

Sheffield is short, shows wavering command, and has battled various injuries over his career, so he's often been tipped as a potential impact reliever instead of a potential impact starter. The Yankees didn't appear all that interested in giving him starting reps, passing him over for promotions repeatedly in favor of lesser prospects over the past two seasons. He's now landed in a situation where he will get every opportunity to start over the next few years. The delta is a bit higher than you'd expect for a basically ready upper-minors arm, but with that does come higher upside than most of his cohort.

The Risks: Medium, although there's positive risk here too. If Sheffield can stay in the rotation, increase the consistency of his changeup and command, and avoid injuries, he does have high-end starting potential. But there are a lot of command and durability questions. If this all sounds like the guy he got traded for, well, it might be.

Bret Sayre's Fantasy Take: I really wish I felt better about Sheffield's chances of sticking in a rotation, but even though I'm skeptical, the sneaky SP2 upside gives him plenty of value in dynasty leagues. Of course, it helps that he's slated to throw 120-plus innings this year. The stuff is there for him to strike out 10 batters per nine as a starter and more as a reliever, but the ratios could hold him back due to said command issues. From a purely statistical standpoint, he's got Mike Clevinger upside but without the hair.

2. Jarred Kelenic   OF

OFP: 60   Likely: 50   ETA: 2021
Born: 07/16/99   Age: 19   Bats: L   Throws: L   Height: 6'1"   Weight: 196
Origin: Round 1, 2018 Draft (#6 overall)

The Report: Kelenic has more present skills than you might expect from a cold-weather prep bat. The background, drafting organization, and draft position are going to elicit Brandon Nimmo comps as he moves through the minors, but Kelenic is a much more polished product than Nimmo was at 19. He's a better bet to stick as at least an average center fielder too. He can really go get it on the grass, with good instincts and the ability to adjust his routes on the fly. The only thing he really lacks is explosive closing speed on balls, although he is a plus runner at present and I don't see his already mature frame filling out much more.

At the plate Kelenic shows above-average bat speed, covers velo well, and the ball jumps off his bat with backspin. He can get a little handsy during his load and lose some bat control, and the swing will get long at times. He can be exploited early in counts, as he likes to hunt fastballs early. There isn't anything here that screams future plus tool—outside of his arm, which has gotten plus-plus grades thrown on it as an amateur—but all five clock in at average-or-better. That's a nice package in a center field prospect.

The Risks: High. Kelenic hasn't played above rookie-ball yet, and there are some "tweener" warning signs in the profile.

Bret Sayre's Fantasy Take: There's a lot to like from a fantasy standpoint, but not a lot to love here, which means he'll have to max out the sum of his parts in order to be a cornerstone outfielder. He has the potential to hit for average (near .300 if it all clicks), tap into 20-homer power, and steal 20-plus bases, yet the odds of him doing all three are small. He's still a very solid OF3 in the long run if two of those three come together, and he has the potential to move quickly for a prep bat due to his advanced approach. Still, Kelenic found himself on the outside looking in at my top-10 2018 signees and that'll probably be the case on the 101 as well.

3. Evan White 1B

OFP: 60   Likely: 50   ETA: 2020
Born: 04/26/96   Age: 23   Bats: R   Throws: L   Height: 6'3"   Weight: 205
Origin: Round 1, 2017 Draft (#17 overall)

The Report: White's a weird profile, and thus a fun player. The ol' right-hit, left-throw trick's a tough one to pull off, especially for collegiate first basemen who lack prototypical first-base game pop. There's always been plenty of well-founded optimism about the hit tool, and for evident reason: he sees the ball well, works counts effectively, and capably rifles line drives to all fields. There's good torque and bat speed off a deep load, and he's athletic enough to stay back that extra beat and still sync things up to fire at a pitch on time. The club implemented some swing changes over the course of the season to get his legs more involved and help him generate a plane more conducive to lifting and driving pitches, and he did just that down the stretch.

The athleticism is top-shelf for the cold corner. He moves with grace and fluidity around the bag, receives throws with soft hands, and combines quickness, agility, and supreme body control to get after hot hoppers hit his way. He's an efficient runner with a surprising burst, and the body should hang on to above-average or better speed for the foreseeable future. The Mariners have thus far resisted the obvious temptation to create reps for him in the outfield, but it seems an inevitable outcome in today's game, and he certainly presents the physicality of someone capable of meeting the demands of multiple positions. If it all comes together he can evolve into a versatile player capable of adding value in all three phases of the game.

The Risks: Low but also high? It's complicated. Whether the swing changes and subsequent power burst all holds will have a lot to say about where on the spectrum of a given 25-man roster he winds up. It's really strange to talk about any first baseman's glove as something that sets a reasonably high floor for him, but White's is really, really good, so here we are.

Bret Sayre's Fantasy Take: This is like the profile you would have written for Eric Hosmer nearly a decade ago if you knew he wasn't going to take that step forward in power. And that's not to say Hosmer hasn't been valuable—he's had a few impressive campaigns, sometimes on the back of his thefts and sometimes on the back of a friendly BABIP—yet this is a tough fantasy profile to rely on without a more extreme hit tool. Unfortunately, White's hit tool isn't enough to make him more than a top-150 dynasty prospect.

4. Justin Dunn RHP

OFP: 55 Likely: 45 ETA: Late 2019
Born: 09/22/95 Age: 23 Bats: R Throws: R Height: 6'2" Weight: 185
Origin: Round 1, 2016 Draft (#19 overall)

The Report: After command issues led to a bit of a lost 2017 in the Florida State League, Dunn looked more like a first-round arm in 2018. He still hasn't consistently shown 95+ velocity as a starter in the pros, more often touching 95 while sitting in the average velocity band. The heater can run a little true, showing occasional riding life or cut, but lacking the explosive armside movement he had coming out of BC. The slider projects as above-average, a mid-80s offering with good, late tilt. Dunn's worked on a curveball more this year, but it is difficult to tease out from the slider at times, and he tends to cast it, making it a bit of a slurvy, 11-4 roller. The changeup is still used sparingly and tends to be too firm, although he will usually show one or two a start with good tumble.

Dunn has an athletic delivery, but lacks plane as he's on the short side and uses a three-quarters slot. He throws across his body as well, limiting his command projection to averageish. Dunn has the arsenal to start, but looks more like an "average starter" type, and he might have more impact in relief.

The Risks: Medium. Dunn's had some Double-A success, but there's significant reliever risk here without further command and third pitch gains.

Bret Sayre's Fantasy Take: There's only about a 30-40 percent chance that Dunn becomes even a usable mixed-league starting pitcher, let alone a solid SP4 as further development might portend. There are worse places to work if you don't have a true out pitch against lefties than T-Mobile, but Dunn barely registers as a top-200 name at this point and his movement to the Mariners decreases my confidence that he'll make good on that first-round promise.

5. Logan Gilbert RHP

OFP: 55 Likely: 45 ETA: Late 2020
Born: 05/05/97 Age: 22 Bats: R Throws: R Height: 6'6" Weight: 225
Origin: Round 1, 2018 Draft (#14 overall)

The Report: Stetson University doesn't always produce major-league arms, but when they do, they are Cy Young winners (well, and Lenny Dinardo). Gilbert doesn't have deGrom or Kluber-level stuff, but neither did those two coming out of college (his flow has deGrom potential though). What Gilbert does have is a big

6-foot-8 frame that belies a fairly easy delivery, and a fastball that touches 95. He changes eye levels well with the heater and there is some run and sink at times as well.

Gilbert has a full four-pitch mix, and the curve is his most advanced offering. It flashes plus with tight 12-5 break, but will get loose and humpy at times as well. The slider and change are both potentially average. He does a good job of staying online with his delivery despite a huge frame, but he can get a little "tall and fall" and his command wavers. Gilbert also has yet to throw a pro pitch because he was shut down with mononucleosis. That's a new one.

The Risks: Medium. Gilbert is the kind of polished college arm that usually moves through the minors quickly. "Usually." We have no evidence of that yet though.

Bret Sayre's Fantasy Take: If there's a profile I just genuinely mistrust, it's the tall pitcher without overpowering stuff profile. Give me a tall pitcher who can touch triple-digits and I'll painfully wait through the Tyler Glasnow's of the world, but I'm not inclined to stick around to find out if a pitcher with pretty good stuff figures out of how make use of his long levers. I would not look to him with a second- or third-round pick in dynasty drafts this year, as the odds he gets to his SP4 upside aren't as good as they need to be.

6 Erik Swanson   RHP   OFP: 55   Likely: 45   ETA: 2019
Born: 09/04/93   Age: 25   Bats: R   Throws: R   Height: 6'3"   Weight: 235
Origin: Round 8, 2014 Draft (#246 overall)

The Report: Not all that long ago, this was one of my favorite sleeper pitching prospects. He's officially too high-profile now to really be called a sleeper, traded twice in significant deals and on the fringes of the 101 discussion, if ultimately a half-grade low. But he might be a pretty good pitcher pretty soon.

Because Swanson—now 25, and in his sixth pro season—has taken some time to ripen as a prospect due to injuries and late development, we think his stuff has been undersold a bit. His fastball can sit as high as the mid-90s and touches 98, and the pitch has plane and life to it. He also throws a hard slider that we like, a developing changeup, and the occasional curveball. He's generally shown strong command and control throughout the minors. He has a big, sturdy-looking frame and looks pretty clean in his delivery, but he's battled injuries over the course of his career and doesn't always hold his velocity through starts. Ultimately, the stuff might pop more in relief.

In other organizations, we suspect Swanson would've gotten a chance during the 2018 season, but the Yankees are perpetually loaded with pitching and always have a crowded 40-man situation. Swanson is now on the 40-man, and Mariners general manager Jerry Dipoto pronounced Swanson as "major-league ready" following the trade. Like Sheffield, he will get every chance to work out in Seattle's rotation over the next few years.

The Risks: Medium. Swanson has a decent amount of relief/injury risk, and has also been generally on the older side for his leagues.

Bret Sayre's Fantasy Take: The argument for Swanson, like Sheffield before him, is centered around his proximity, but accounts for sneaky upside if he can make it through the gauntlet of a full major-league season as a starter. While Swanson may be more SP4 than SP2, he still offers 180-plus-strikeout potential and the ability to register an above-average WHIP. He should be owned in all leagues that roster 200 prospects.

7. Shed Long 2B
OFP: 55 Likely: 45 ETA: Late 2019
Born: 08/22/95 Age: 23 Bats: L Throws: R Height: 5'8" Weight: 184
Origin: Round 12, 2013 Draft (#375 overall)

The Report: After struggling some in his initial pass through the Southern League in 2017, Long had a successful consolidation year in 2018. He lacks a standout tool, but he does everything well enough. There's still a bit more swing and miss here than you'd like—Long will do the short-hitter thing where he thinks he can hit pitches at his throat—which may make the hit and power tools only play to average. Long is a good athlete though and still an above-average runner despite the squarish physique. He's fine at second, and could handle a few other spots on the grass or dirt if he's ultimately a bench-piece. But even with the glut of talent at the keystone nowadays, averagish tools across the board are still nice to have at an up-the-middle spot.

The Risks: Medium. It's possible the swing-and-miss issues continue to get worse against better pitching, but there's a broad enough base of skills here to expect some sort of major-league career.

Bret Sayre's Fantasy Take: This was a much more attractive offensive profile before middle infielders started going bananas with the bats. Yet Long continues to trudge along as a potential top-15 second baseman, capable of 15 homers and 15 steals. It's possible GABP could help him sneak beyond the 20 mark in a season or two, but that will likely be the only time he's more than a good MI option in 12-15 team mixed leagues.

8. Kyle Lewis OF
OFP: 55 Likely: 45 ETA: 2020
Born: 07/13/95 Age: 23 Bats: R Throws: R Height: 6'4" Weight: 210
Origin: Round 1, 2016 Draft (#11 overall)

The Report: The greatest success story of Lewis' season was that he had a season at all. It still wasn't a full season, mind you, but it was one that saw him return to more or less full health by the end of it. And that counts for a lot. He's missed a spectacular amount of developmental time battling terrible things in his knee, and the learning curve is only going to get steeper in the months ahead. But the raw tools that got him drafted 11th overall remain readily apparent. He's strong as an ox, with all-fields power and thunder off the barrel. The straight-line speed and elite explosiveness aren't quite there anymore, but the physicality and twitch still are, and the instincts to make those attributes play defensively are, too. It probably makes more sense for everybody if they shuffle him over to right sooner or later, but there's still a shot he can spell up the middle. The bat still has a long road ahead: he struggles to recognize spin, and he'll expand accordingly when fooled. Velocity up can still bite him. But he can catch the latter and leave the junk alone, and the baseball acumen has long been understood as an asset. It's about health and reps now, and he'll need a lot of both to swallow up the kind of growth he's missed and will need.

The Risks: High. He's got a lot of work to catch up on, and the structural integrity of his knee will remain a gaping question mark until it isn't.

Bret Sayre's Fantasy Take: Lewis, at this point in pro career, has both the upside and the knee structure of a 31-year-old Adam Jones and that was not the ceiling that was promised when he was drafted. Yet, like Jones, the bat can still make up for it. Lewis could develop into a .270 hitter with 25 bombs for as long as he can stay on the field, but *could* carries a lot of weight here.

9. Julio Rodriguez   OF

OFP: 55   Likely: 40   ETA: 2023
Born: 12/29/00   Age: 18   Bats: R   Throws: R   Height: 6'3"   Weight: 180
Origin: International Free Agent, 2017

The Report: The Mariners signed Rodriguez for $1,750,000 out of the Dominican in July 2017 on the strength of his power stroke. He slugged .500+ in the Dominican Summer League last year, which is at least marginally better than not doing that. There's some length to the swing, but Rodriguez could have plus-plus raw power at maturity with a decent shot to get most of it into games. He's got plenty of arm for right field, which is good because he's already a right fielder at 17. That's less good; you like to at least pretend your top IFAs can play up the middle in their teenage years. Obviously that puts a lot of pressure on the bat, and there's still some uncertainty on how Rodriguez's frame will develop into his 20s. Because he's 17. It's the prototypical right field prospect profile, but with even more risk and uncertainty than your average good right field prospect.

The Risks: Extreme. He's 17, already a right fielder, and not yet stateside.

Bret Sayre's Fantasy Take: This is going to take a while, but man is there a lot to like about Rodriguez's bat. He's got the raw power to hit 30-plus bombs and was reasonably advanced as one of the young-uns in the DSL, especially with the hit tool. You can dream of a 6/7 future here, and while there's plenty of downside from there, Rodriguez probably has the highest potential in this system. He's a sneaky name to invest in this year if he's not owned in your dynasty league—presuming you roster 200+ prospects.

Seattle Mariners 2019

10 **Sam Carlson RHP** OFP: 55 Likely: 40 ETA: 2022 or 2023
Born: 12/03/98 Age: 20 Bats: R Throws: R Height: 6'4" Weight: 195
Origin: Round 2, 2017 Draft (#55 overall)

The Report: Carlson missed all of 2018 after undergoing Tommy John surgery early in the year. He's likely to miss a fair bit of 2019 as well. When healthy, he was considered a bit of a steal in the second round of the 2017 draft. He's a cold-weather prep arm who popped a few extra ticks on radar guns his senior year and he offers a projectable slider as well. We will see what comes back after rehab, but given the lower slot and high effort delivery, the odds that he's a reliever have only gone up.

The Risks: Extreme. He's in the midst of Tommy John recovery and has three professional innings to his name.

Bret Sayre's Fantasy Take: Carlson was one of my favorite prep pitchers out of the 2017 draft, but this detour just means he'll be available on waivers if he returns in 2020 and starts shoving in full-season ball. Don't burn a roster spot until then.

The Next Five:

11 **Braden Bishop OF**
Born: 08/22/93 Age: 25 Bats: R Throws: R Height: 6'1" Weight: 190
Origin: Round 3, 2015 Draft (#94 overall)

Bishop was keeping on keeping on, until a pitch fractured his forearm and ended his 2018 season early. The profile here is the same as it was last year, a speed and defense center fielder with questions about how the bat will play against better arms. Double-A is the first real test against "better arms" and Bishop was fine in the Texas League, despite a handsy swing that can limit the quality of his contact at times. He has below-average power at best, but perhaps with enough OBP to carry a second-division starter profile. The clock is ticking some on Bishop—who is already 25—but assuming he comes back from his forearm injury with minimal lingering issues, the Mariners will certainly have major-league outfield openings in 2019. And as a potential plus center fielder, his C.V. stands out in a shallow system.

12 **Damon Casetta-Stubbs RHP**
Born: 07/22/99 Age: 19 Bats: R Throws: R Height: 6'4" Weight: 200
Origin: Round 11, 2018 Draft (#328 overall)

The Mariners system is better (read: not the worst), but yeah, an overslot 11th round prep righty still clocks in here. That's not quite as bad as it sounds on paper. His velocity trended up his senior year and he's regularly in the mid-90s now. His slider is a potential plus pitch, and there's some feel for a changeup. The mechanics are going to need some smoothing out, and he looks very much like a fastball/slider reliever at present given the uptempo delivery and lower slot. He's only 19 though, and there is upside worth monitoring.

13 Cal Raleigh C
Born: 11/26/96   Age: 22   Bats: B   Throws: R   Height: 6'3"   Weight: 215
Origin: Round 3, 2018 Draft (#90 overall)

The Mariners third-round pick in the 2018 draft, Raleigh is a polished, two-way catcher. While his receiving skills won't have FanGraphs' managing editor erasing Mike Zunino's framing numbers from the cover of her Trapper Keeper any time soon, he's a solid backstop with an average arm who's more athletic and agile than you'd expect given his size, if a bit slow out of a crouch. At the plate Raleigh offers above-average bat speed and potential plus power. An ACC catcher beating up the Northwest League isn't anything out of the ordinary, but the path to playing time behind the plate in Seattle is, uh, clearer now, and Raleigh's polished bat could get him there quickly if the glove comes along as well.

14 Wyatt Mills RHP
Born: 01/25/95   Age: 24   Bats: R   Throws: R   Height: 6'3"   Weight: 175
Origin: Round 3, 2017 Draft (#93 overall)

Mills looks like your typical sidearming righty, beating up on the low minors by throwing from an angle these poor kids haven't seen before. That's not really the narrative here though. First off, all these kids have been seeing low slot dudes for a while; most college and low minors teams have at least two. And Mills' stuff is anything but typical for that profile. He can dial his fastball up to 93 with sink and run, and his low-80s slider should end up above-average or better. The two pitches look the same out of his hand, and he throws strikes with both. There might even be enough changeup to crossover, although Mills' tends to be even flatter than the heater. He has to live at the edges of the zones, and a Double-A cameo showed that better hitters make for finer margins, but there's still a potential Steve Cishekish outcome here, and that's a top-15 prospect in this system.

15 Matt Festa RHP
Born: 03/11/93   Age: 26   Bats: R   Throws: R   Height: 6'2"   Weight: 195
Origin: Round 7, 2016 Draft (#207 overall)

Festa became the second East Stroudsburg Warrior to toe a big-league bump when he debuted last June, and he should be in the mix for the middle innings in the year ahead. He more or less abandoned his second breaker, a curveball, on the biggest stage, in favor of a hard four-seam/slider combo. A strong drive and whippy arm action help him propel those pitches effectively to the lower quadrants, and while the velocity backed up a tick last season he's still got plenty of it to get under barrels effectively in the middle innings. The slider has solid late action that minor-league hitters have consistently struggled to find, and if it plays similarly there's a chance for higher-leverage utility here. Is it the sexiest profile in town? No. Could we have waxed poetic in this space about Dan Vogelbach crushing Triple A and knocking on the door of what should finally be a legitimate shot at regular big-league at-bats? Yes. Yes, we could have.

Top Talents 25 and Under (born 4/1/93 or later):

1. J.P. Crawford
2. Justus Sheffield
3. Jarred Kelenic
4. Mallex Smith
5. Evan White
6. Justin Dunn
7. Logan Gilbert
8. Erik Swanson
9. Kyle Lewis
10. Julio Rodriguez

The kids are alriiiight? I guess? This list obviously looks a lot like the names above, and when your prospect list is bottom-third in baseball it's... it's not great. That the only two non-prospects among this group are brand-new acquisitions made this offseason should tell you all you need to know about the organization's recent operating philosophy.

There was a time, not that long ago and across multiple off-seasons, when J.P. Crawford was one of the best prospects in all the land. We comped him to Jimmy Rollins in 2016, and he remained a 7/6-lookin' prospect as recently as our 2017 list iteration. The bat has stalled at the upper echelons of minor-league ball, wet-blanketed further in its development last year by multiple trips to the DL and inconsistent opportunity to test his mettle against the biggest boys. He made some encouraging tweaks in the homestretch, and nothing about the physicality or actions suggests he doesn't still have time to take anticipated strides forward. The Mariners are certainly banking on it after shipping one of their most valuable players to obtain his services.

For his part, Mallex Smith put together a top-line breakout campaign in Tampa last year, albeit one that looked a little less impressive once you climb under the hood. The batting average and stolen-base proclivity may have wowed fantasy baseballers far and wide, but DRC+ was much less impressed with what it deemed a below-average performance at the dish, while defensive metrics roundly agreed that Smith was not a helpful center fielder on balance. On the latter point, he's still young and fast, and defensive metrics are what they are. And on the former, it was a fun, hopefully stepping-stone style offensive campaign for a player in his first season of full-time duty. Another step forward in his development is possible, and the M's are currently committing a significant chunk of their young-player pot to the hope that he takes it.

Part 3: Featured Articles

The Hole in The Shift is Fixing Itself

Russell Carleton

I've been on a bit of a mission against The Shift of late. I'm not out to get The Shift for the usual reasons that people oppose it. The words "the right way to play the game" won't be found on my lips. If a team wants to pursue a strategy that is within the rules and it works, then by all means, they have my blessing (not that they need it). Instead, my concern with The Shift is a worry that it doesn't work, or at least that it has a flaw that needs fixing.

The data show that while The Shift does a decent job of preventing singles on balls in play (what it's supposed to do), it also increases the number of walks that happen in front of it, and the number of additional walks outweighs the number of singles saved. It's a problem because you can't throw a guy out if he gets to walk to first base.

But the "why" was important. It seemed that The Shift was changing the way in which pitchers pitched. We saw that there were fewer fastballs thrown in front of The Shift than we might otherwise expect, and that pitchers tended to stay out of the strike zone a little more. Not by a lot. In fact, it might not even be visible to the naked eye. The percentage of pitches that are out of the zone goes from 51.0 to 53.3 from a standard defense (two right/two left) to a full shift (three on one side). That difference stands up even after we control for the types of hitters that get shifted against. And it's enough to drive up the walk rate to where it cancels out the benefits that teams thought they were getting with The Shift... and then some.

But there was some hope. I found that when individual pitchers stayed closer to the in-zone/out-of-zone mix that they used without The Shift on, they could still get the benefits of The Shift without the walk problems. So, in theory, a team could simply figure out a way to convince its pitchers to not fall prey to the walk trap and The Shift would once again be their friend.

It's reasonable to think that some teams might be more hip to this idea than others. Maybe some figured it out a year before the others. Maybe they were better at getting the message across to their pitchers. Or, maybe no one has figured it out yet.

Warning! Gory Mathematical Details Ahead!

Seattle Mariners 2019

I used data from 2015-2017, made available through MLB's data portal, Baseball Savant. They are kind enough to note when teams are using an infield shift (three fielders on one side of second base), as opposed to a "strategic shift" (someone's playing a bit out of position, but it's not quite that drastic) or a "standard" alignment.

Since we're doing this by team, I can't just look at raw walk rates, because we know that some teams have good pitchers and others have not-so-good pitchers. Some have a mix of both. I used the log-odds ratio method to take into account a batter's general walking proclivities, and a pitcher's as well, and then shoving them into a binary logistic regression. Then, I asked the computer to generate a specific coefficient for each team's pitchers, for when they went into The Shift and how that affected their walk rate.

Using those coefficients, I was able to project what would happen if a league-average pitcher faced a league-average hitter (which we expect would product a league-average walk rate; from 2015-2017, 7.7 percent of plate appearances ended in a walk) and then just switched his hat. Here's the top five and the bottom five:

Top 5 Teams	Projected Shift Walk Rate	Bottom 5 Teams	Projected Shift Walk Rate
Rockies	6.2%	Rangers	11.2%
Pirates	6.7%	Mets	10.4%
Indians	7.2%	Dodgers	10.2%
Astros	7.3%	Cardinals	9.9%
Braves	7.7%	Tigers	9.7%

There are probably people out there right now trying to figure out what the common thread is among the top and bottom teams. I'm sure, because this is Baseball Prospectus, people are already trying to make the case that sabermetric "early adopters" have some sort of edge here. I think that the more interesting piece is that by the time you get to fifth place in The Shift, we're at league average.

As a sanity check, I examined the issue on a pitch-by-pitch level, looking at how often pitchers threw their pitches in the GameDay strike zone, and again using the same basic methodology and getting team-specific coefficients. The names on the list re-arranged themselves, but the idea was the same, and the two lists correlated with an R of .593.

There's a reason that I don't usually do this type of leaderboard post. I don't really know what the Rockies, Pirates, Indians, Astros, and Braves have in common, or what they have that the bottom five don't. I can put a shrug emoji here and say, "Well, it must be something!" but that seems like a cop-out. Instead, I'd like to present another table and suggest that the table above doesn't even really matter anymore.

Year	League Percent Outside K Zone (Full Shift)	League Percent in K Zone (No Shift)	Difference
2015	54.1%	51.1%	3.0%
2016	53.3%	50.9%	2.4%
2017	52.6%	50.9%	1.7%
2018	52.0%	50.7%	1.3%

The hole in The Shift is fixing itself, and it's coming down really fast league wide. In my earlier work on The Shift, I suggested that until teams stopped having such a huge difference between their out-of-zone rate with and without The Shift on, there would just be too many walks for The Shift to make sense. It seems that all 30 of them have been working toward just that. I once estimated that it takes about 10 years for an idea to filter its way through baseball. At this rate, it looks like teams are going to catch up a lot faster than that. And yeah, they're all saber-smart now.

It's likely that whatever magic it was that the Rockies and Pirates had has made its way to Texas and Queens. Or is at least on its way. And if teams are committing to fixing the walk problem, then it's likely that they will continue shifting and shifting a lot.

And eventually it's going to actually make sense for them to do it.

—*Russell Carleton is a former author of Baseball Prospectus and now an analyst for the New York Mets.*

The State of the Quality Start

Rob Mains

One of the seven things you (probably) didn't know about the 2018 season is that quality starts—defined as a start lasting six or more innings with three or fewer earned runs allowed—as a percentage of total starts cratered to an all-time low of 41 percent. I want to look a little more deeply into this, since it's been a while (May of 2016, to be exact) since I've examined quality starts.

The term *quality start* is credited to *Philadelphia Inquirer* sportswriter John Lowe. It's been derided ever since he coined it in December of 1985. Three runs in six innings? That's a 4.50 ERA! In what world is that a measure of quality?

Let's start with that criticism. It's true that 3 x 9 / 6 = 4.5. (You came here for this sort of high-level math, right?) But it's also true that type of start, meeting the bare minimum for earning a quality start, is unusual. Here's the proportion of quality starts in which the pitcher lasted exactly six innings and yielded exactly three earned runs. (I'm going to confine this analysis to the 30-team era, 1998-present. Almost all data retrieved in this article is via the Baseball-Reference Play Index.)

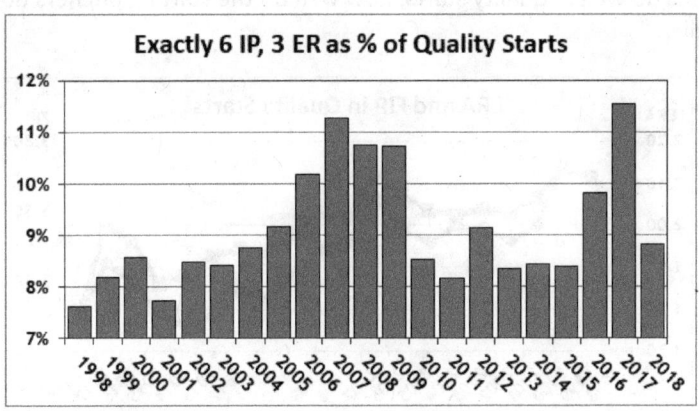

There were 1,997 quality starts in 2018. Only 176, or fewer than one in 11, featured a pitcher going six innings and allowing three earned runs. Put another way, the percentage of quality starts that resulted in a 4.50 ERA (8.8 percent) is less than half the percentage of games in which a batter hit two home runs and his team lost (22.5 percent; 237-69 won-lost). That doesn't impugn hitting two homers.

So if a 4.50 ERA isn't the norm, what is? How good are quality starts?

Pretty good, it turns out. First, on a team level:

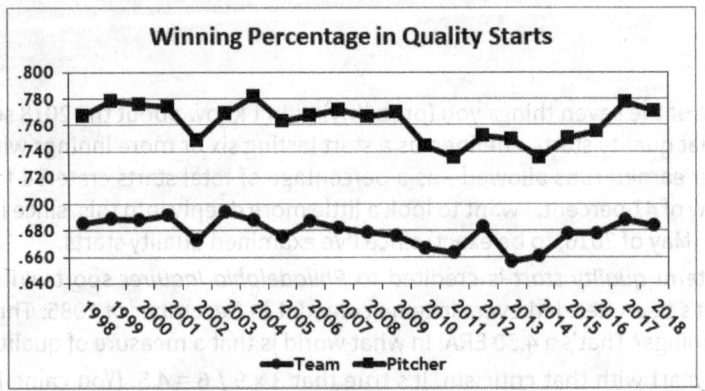

Teams receiving a quality start from their pitcher won 68.4 percent of their games in 2018, in line with the 30-team era average of 67.9 percent. A team with a .684 winning percentage wins 111 games. Getting a quality start is definitely a good thing. Individual pitchers throwing quality starts have a higher winning percentage because a big slice of team losses is assigned to a reliever.

If teams do well in quality starts, how well do the starting pitchers do? Again, very well.

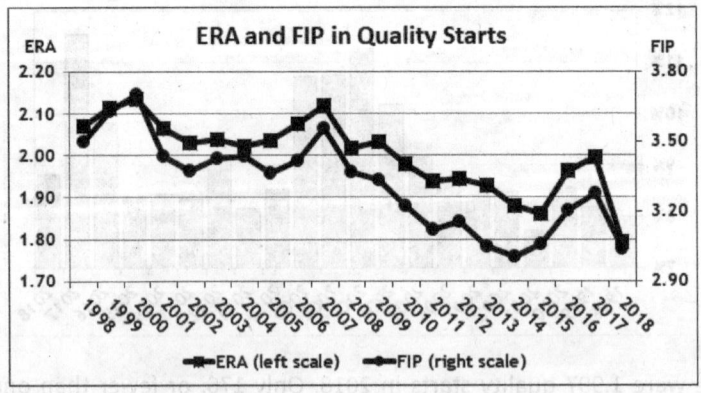

Pitchers in quality starts had a 1.79 ERA (blue line) in 2018, *the lowest in the 30-team era*. Their FIP was higher, 3.04, but still excellent. In the 30-team era, only 2014 had a lower FIP for quality starts, 3.01.

But, of course, the run environment in 2014 was different. Teams in 2014 scored 4.07 runs per game, the fewest in a non-strike year since 1976. They scored 4.45 runs per game in 2018. So surrendering a 3.04 FIP in 2018 is more impressive than 3.01 in 2014. Accordingly, let's look at ERA and FIP in quality starts relative to league averages.

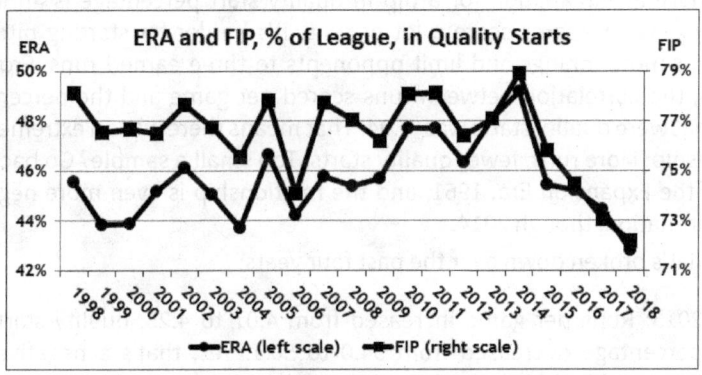

This tells a more dramatic story. Starting pitchers in 2018 gave up a 4.19 ERA and a 4.21 FIP. Starters in quality starts gave up a 1.79 ERA, 43 percent of the league average. Starters in quality starts gave up a 3.04 FIP, 72 percent of the league average. Both of these marks represent lows in the 30-team era.

The takeaway here is this: *Quality starts are better, relative to other starts, than they've ever been over the past 21 years.*

Maybe during the winter I'll look at this over a longer arc of time. For now, though, we can definitively say quality starts are the best they've ever been since the Diamondbacks and Rays joined the majors.

Yet, paradoxically, they're down.

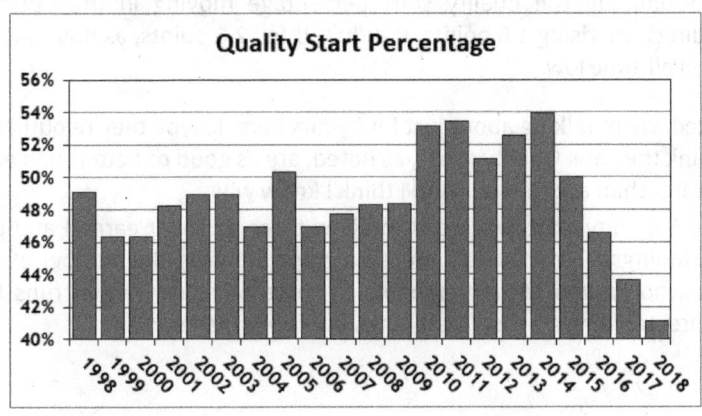

This graph covers only the 30-team era. In my article last week, though, I looked at the years 1908-2018. The result was the same. The 41 percent of starts in 2018 that were quality starts are an all-time low, well below the runners-up: 1930's 43 percent (the year teams scored an all-time record 5.55 runs per game) and last year's 44 percent.

The normal explanation for a dip in quality start percentage is an increase in scoring. When teams score a lot of runs, it's harder for starting pitchers to last six or more innings and limit opponents to three earned runs. From 1998 to 2014, the correlation between runs scored per game and the percentage of starts that were quality starts was -0.94. That means there was an extremely close relationship: More runs, fewer quality starts. Too small a sample? Go back to the start of the Expansion Era, 1961, and the relationship is even more negative, a -0.95 correlation, though 2014.

But that's broken down over the past four years:

- 2015: Runs per game increased from 4.07 to 4.25, quality start percentage decreased from 54.0 to 50.1. Yes, that's a negative relationship, but the regression model would predict a decline of 1.5 percentage points. We got 3.9 instead.
- 2016: Runs per game increased from 4.25 to 4.48, quality start percentage decreased from 50.1 to 46.6. Past experience would suggest a decline of just 1.8 percentage points. We got 3.4.
- 2017: Runs per game increased from 4.48 to 4.65, quality start percentage decreased from 46.6 to 43.6. Again, the direction's right, but the magnitude isn't. Using the relationship from 1998 to 2014, that increase in scoring should've reduced quality starts by 1.3 percentage points, not 2.9.
- 2018: Runs per game declined from 4.65 to 4.45. That should've resulted in the quality start percentage moving in the other direction, rising 1.6 points. It didn't. It fell 2.6 points, as noted, to an all-time low.

Granted, we're talking about just four years here. Maybe they're outliers. But I don't think they are. Quality starts, as noted, are as good or better than ever. But they're rarer than ever as well. And I think I know why.

To get a quality start, you need to allow three or fewer earned and pitch at least six innings. That's 18 outs. Here's a graph showing the number of starting pitchers who limited their opponents to three or fewer earned runs but got pulled after pitching at least five innings but fewer than six:

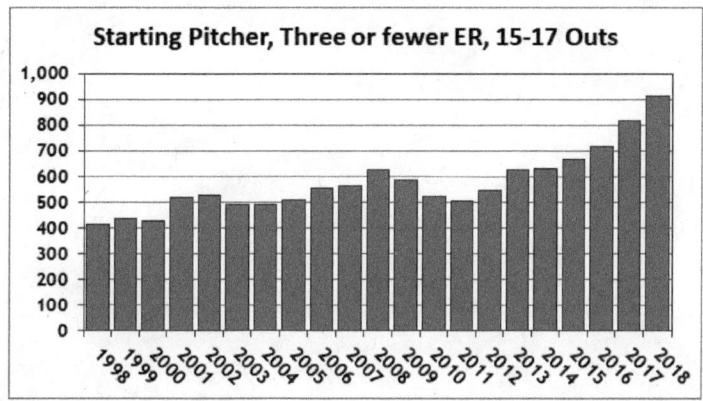

A pitcher getting 15 outs pitched five innings. A pitcher getting 16 outs pitched 5 1/3. A pitcher getting 17 outs pitched 5 2/3. More than ever before, pitchers are being removed from games in which they are within 1-3 outs of a quality start, falling just short of the six-inning finish line. Widespread acknowledgement of the times-through-the-order penalty and a flotilla of available bullpen arms is making the quality start simultaneously both more excellent and more rare.

Which is ironic, given that we saw a new post-war quality start record this season:

Rank	Pitcher	Season	Consecutive QS
1	Jacob deGrom	2018	24
2	Bob Gibson	1968	22
-	Chris Carpenter	2005	22
4	Johan Santana	2004	21
5	Luis Tiant	1968	20
-	Mike Scott	1986	20
-	Jake Arrieta	2015	20
8	Robin Roberts	1952	19
-	Tom Seaver	1973	19
-	Jack Morris	1983	19
-	Greg Maddux	1998	19
-	Josh Johnson	2010	19
-	Jon Lester	2014	19

While there have been longer streaks spread over multiple seasons, no pitcher since World War II threw more consecutive quality starts in one year than Jacob deGrom this year. The fact that he did in a year in which quality starts were the rarest they've ever been adds to the accomplishment.

—*Rob Mains is an author of Baseball Prospectus.*

Heads-Up Hacking—The First Pitch

Matthew Trueblood

Batters fell behind in a higher percentage of all plate appearances in 2018 than in any previous season for which we have pitch-by-pitch data. That kind of granular information goes back only to 1988, but we might safely assume (given all we know about baseball as it had been before that, and as it has been in the years since) that batters have *never* fallen behind at a higher rate than they did last season.

Through the 1990s, the percentage of all plate appearances that began 0-1 hovered in the high 30s and low 40s. In the 2000s, it rose steadily but slowly, through the mid-40s. In 2018, 49.8 percent of all trips to the plate began 0-1. That, as much as anything, captures in microcosm the nature of hitting in MLB today.

A countdown clock toward strike three begins ticking almost the moment a batter takes his place in the box. The league's adjusted OPS+ on the first pitch was higher in 2018 than ever before, and that has been true in most of the last 10 seasons. Batters hit .264/.289/.442 in all plate appearances in which they swung at the first pitch last season, and .241/.330/.395 in all plate appearances in which they took that first offering.

The percentage differences in batting average and isolated power there favor swinging at the first pitch by more than in any season since 1988, while the difference in on-base percentage favors taking by more than ever. If you want to get on base at a decent clip, it's a good idea to be patient, but you run the risk of missing the only chances you'll get to produce power.

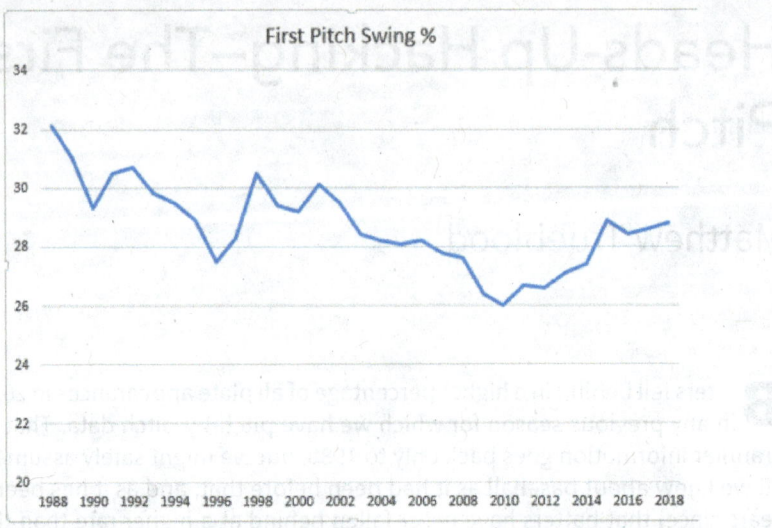

The league swung at the first pitch 28.8 percent of the time in 2018. With the isolated exception of 2015, that's the highest that number has climbed since 2002, but it might not be high enough. With the help of BP research maven Rob McQuown, I looked at the aggregate Called Strike Probability (CSProb) on the first pitch for each season since 2008, when the implementation of PITCHf/x first made measuring that possible. It's risen sharply during that period.

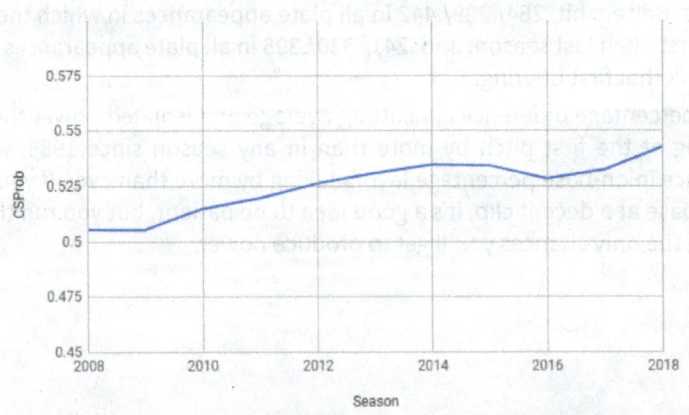

Called Strike Probability, First Pitch of PA (2008-2018)

Called Strike Probability is exactly what it sounds like: a pitch with a given CSProb has roughly that chance of being called a strike, if not swung at. In 2018, a batter who took 100 first pitches from a random sampling of the league's pitchers might expect to fall behind 54 or 55 times—up from 50 or 51 times in 2008. Almost regardless of pitch type (and, notably, especially in the case of fastballs), the first pitch tends to have more of the zone right now than ever before.

Pitchers are better at throwing strikes. They have better stuff, and believe more in their ability to miss bats within the zone. Perhaps most importantly, they know that batters are looking for one thing on the first pitch: a fastball. If they don't get it, they're likely to take the pitch. Check out how the use of sinkers and four-seamers on the first pitch has changed in a decade:

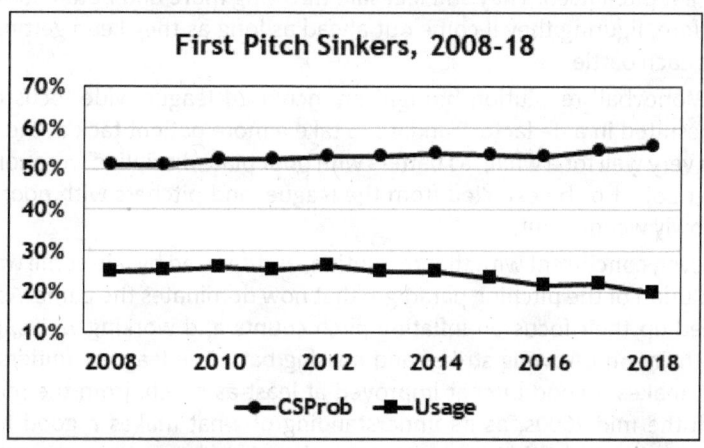

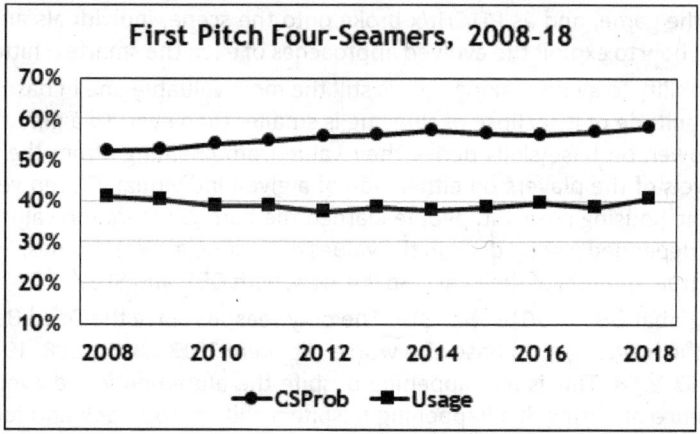

Heads-Up Hacking—The First Pitch - 109

Seattle Mariners 2019

The sinker is losing its place in baseball, but the rate at which pitchers have thrown it on the first pitch hasn't dropped any faster than its usage rate in other counts. Pitchers have actually gone to their four-seamer *more* often to open counts, in the last few years, after a dip in the 2012-2015 period. What's really changed, though, and what shows up in both charts above, is that pitchers are catching more of the zone with first-pitch fastballs than they were a decade ago, or a half-decade ago. They're attacking right away, even with the pitch they know batters are expecting. The message is pretty clear: batters are being too passive.

Sliders, curves, and changeups each have more of the zone when thrown on the first pitch than they did several years ago, too, though the effect is less pronounced. Pitchers have seen the numbers; they know batters are doing better on the first pitch itself. They still feel safe throwing more and better strikes than ever before, figuring they'll come out ahead as long as they keep getting ahead to open each battle.

The Moneyball revolution brought an increased league-wide focus on OBP, which resulted in a de facto mandate to take a more patient tack at the plate. It worked very well for a while, as batters with poor plate discipline were compelled to either adjust or be expelled from the league, and pitchers with poor control were slowly weeded out.

However, concurrent with that revolution, and spurred by it in some ways, was the evolution of the pitching paradigm that now dominates the game. As batters ratcheted up their focus on inflating pitch counts and working walks, pitchers honed theirs on throwing strikes and missing bats. The league's understanding of what makes a good pitcher improved at least as much, from the mid-1990s through the mid-2000s, as its understanding of what makes a good hitter. As amphetamines and other performance-enhancing drugs were phased mostly out of the game, and as PITCHf/x broke onto the scene, individuals and teams learned how to exploit the evolved approaches of even the smartest hitters.

The ability to avoid making outs is still the most valuable one in baseball, but the magnitude of its eclipse of slugging is smaller than ever. To a greater extent than power, on-base skills derive their value from chaining—from the on-base skill levels of the players on either side of a given individual. Eleven years ago, when the housing crisis hit, people learned the hard way that the value of their homes depended a good deal on the values of their neighbors' homes. The same wasn't true, though, of their cars. So it is now, with OBP and SLG.

The global OBP in 2018 was .318. The only seasons since the Dead Ball Era in which the league got on base at a worse clip were 2013-2015, 1988, 1971-1972, and 1963-1968. This is all happening despite the aforementioned evolution of the science of hitting. It's happening despite a shift in approach and focus, one that would steer OBP ever higher, if only it were working.

Instead, it's sitting at a low ebb, and while it does so, even guys who get on base often are a little less helpful than they were 10 years ago—or 20, or 40, or 60, or 70, or 80, or 90. They're less helpful, that is, because unless there happen to be three or four other guys in the lineup who get on just as regularly, their contribution is merely to forestall the inevitable. Runs happen, increasingly, when a sudden bang happens, and that means attacking early in the count—because pitchers are sure as hell doing that.

In a league making contact on barely 75 percent of its swings, and a league in which an increasing number of pitchers can throw multiple off-speed pitches for strikes in any count, the only way to consistently generate offense is going to be aggressive. This isn't necessarily true for individuals, like Mookie Betts and Jose Ramirez, who make a lot of contact and have excellent plate discipline, and whose power comes from such natural quickness in a short stroke. Most players have to make tradeoffs, though, whether it be lowering their contact rate or raising their chase rate, in order to consistently make the quality of contact necessary to survive in today's game.

Highest %	Lowest %
Javier Baez – 48.3	Joe Mauer – 4.6
Freddie Freeman – 47.1	Mookie Betts – 9.7
Ozzie Albies – 46.3	Brett Gardner – 10.7
Jose Altuve – 44.2	Jose Ramirez – 12.0
Nick Castellanos – 44.1	Jason Kipnis – 13.8
Joey Gallo – 42.3	Jesus Aguilar – 14.5
Corey Dickerson – 40.9	Xander Bogaerts – 15.8
Salvador Perez – 40.8	Brian Dozier – 16.3
Eddie Rosario – 40.7	Mike Trout – 17.6
Nick Ahmed – 40.4	Yasmani Grandal – 17.6

Top 10 and Bottom 10 Hitters, First-Pitch Swing Rate (2018)

The question isn't which of these lists one prefers, but what they each convey, qualitatively, about the cat-and-mouse game of early-count hitting. Those top five on the left, especially, drive home the fact that for most players, getting aggressive early in the count is now key to keeping strikeout rate down and hitting for power.

For now, the message is: pitchers are coming right after batters with the nastiest stuff they've ever had. Batters had better stop giving away strike one and force hurlers to adjust, or the global OBP crisis is only going to get worse.

—*Matthew Trueblood is an author of Baseball Prospectus.*

A Hymn for the Index Stat

Patrick Dubuque

We survived without computers. I know this, because I remember the day when my dad hooked up his brand-new Atari 400 computer to the back of our 12-inch Magnavox television, and the perfect blue of the memo pad lit up for the first time. I was born just on the edge of that transitional generation, of learning cursive and balancing checkbooks and just doing math all the time, constant manual arithmetic.

It still amazes me. We learned how to sail ships without computers. We learned how to do calculus. We built towers that didn't fall down, most of the time. We engineered catapults to knock them down anyway. We built a robust system of philosophy called "utilitarianism," founded on the principle that the good of an action is evaluated by summing the effects of that action, which is the kind of formula that would make the world's mainframes crash. The whole foundation of statistics as a field is "here's math you could easily do but would die of old age first."

The fact of the matter is that there is too much math in the world to do. There are too many things changing, and too many things too small to notice, for us to handle. At some point, they become too much for the computers to handle as well, which is why we have chaos theory and undetectable earthquakes, but it's not an even fight. At some point, we fall back on intuition, and given how under-equipped we are, we're forced to bestow that intuition with some sort of supernatural superiority, the "gut feeling," that we can't prove because we can only intuit that our intuition is better.

We're all lousy at intuition, and wonderful at lying to ourselves about it. The honest truth is that computers are far better at intuition than we are, because in order to know what feels "off" you have to know what's "on." In order to do that you have to constantly reassess the average of everything, then re-rank your own experience against it.

Test your own, by comparing these three anonymous lines:

Player	G	HR	AVG	OBP	SLG
Player A	156	38	.259	.342	.535
Player B	154	38	.280	.348	.527
Player C	158	38	.266	.343	.509

These all seem like pretty similar players, right? The second one a touch more batted-ball dependent, the third a little less strong, but all pretty good hitters. And you'd be right, about the latter. Not the former.

Here's the breakdown:

- Player A: 1991 Howard Johnson, 141 DRC+
- Player B: 1996 Dean Palmer, 121 DRC+
- Player C: 2018 Giancarlo Stanton, 114 DRC+

Baseball is fortunate to have escaped the seismic shifts of so many other sports, where the talents and performances of other eras are nearly unrecognizable. (And not just other sports: try to explain the greatness of the movie Duck Soup without adjusting for era.) But they're still there, and they're nearly impossible to account for manually, without having to resort to sweeping generalizations like "steroid era" or juiced-ball era" to throw out entire swathes of production.

This is all to say that we should celebrate the index stat, that simple 100-based scale with such a humble aim: just to give context. It's hard to imagine how we lived without them for so long. Sabermetricians have always tried to make their stats look like other stats: True Average mapped to batting average, FIP molded to look like and compare to ERA. It's easy to understand the motivation—these statistics carry an emotional value in them that is hard to resist, as with the .300 hitter and the 2.00 ERA—but even they fall prey to the same loss of scale as their unadjusted counterparts. If a .300 average means different things in different years, does that hold true for a .300 True Average?

Instead, 100 doesn't say anything, except above average or below. And it does it instantly, for every season in every run environment for any statistic we want it to. We should have more index stats: K%+, so we can stop comparing Mike Clevinger's career 9.46 K/9 to Nolan Ryan's 9.55. HBP%+, so we can note that Ron Hunt was getting plunked when nobody else was getting plunked, as opposed to that imitator Brandon Guyer. Some might note how stale these references are and accuse league-adjustment as a backward-looking drive, and this is true. But we're always looking backward, always comparing the new with the expectations already set. The index stat just forces us to be honest.

There's always resistance to a new statistic, especially one so outwardly simple and so internally complex. We tend to stick with what we know, even in the case of formulas that are supposed to tell us what we know. But if your resistance is that it seems too complicated, too counterintuitive, too "black boxy," I encourage you to consider why you feel that way. Because the real world is infinitely more complicated than baseball, where all the pitches go in one basic direction and the baserunners are only allowed to travel in four directions. Baseball statistics based on mixed methodology are almost impossibly intricate. So are skyscrapers and automobiles. That's why we have computers—to take the guesswork out of them.

—*Patrick Dubuque is an author of Baseball Prospectus.*

Index of Names

Altavilla, Dan 44
Armstrong, Shawn 81
Bautista, Gerson 81
Beckham, Tim 20
Bishop, Braden 62, 90
Bradford, Chasen 81
Bruce, Jay 22
Carlson, Sam 71, 90
Casetta-Stubbs, Damon 90
Crawford, J.P. 24
Crismatt, Nabil 81
Curletta, Joey 79
Dunn, Justin 72, 86
Elias, Roenis 81
Encarnacion, Edwin 26
Festa, Matt 73, 91
Filia, Eric 63
Freitas, David 79
Gearrin, Cory 81
Gerber, Joey 81
Gilbert, Logan 74, 86
Gonzales, Marco 46
Gordon, Dee 28
Haniger, Mitch 30
Healy, Ryon 32
Hernandez, Felix 48
Izturis, Cesar 79
Kelenic, Jarred 64, 84
Kikuchi, Yusei 75
Leake, Mike 51
LeBlanc, Wade 53
Lewis, Kyle 65, 88
Liberato, Luis 79
Lobaton, Jose 79
Long, Shed 66, 88
Miller, Ian 79
Mills, Wyatt 76, 91
Milone, Tommy 55
Narvaez, Omar 34
Negron, Kris 79
Povse, Max 81
Querecuto, Juan 79
Raleigh, Cal 67, 91
Rizzo, Joe 79
Rodriguez, Julio 68, 89
Rosscup, Zac 81
Rumbelow, Nick 81
Sanchez, Ricardo 81
Santana, Domingo 36
Seager, Kyle 38
Sheffield, Justus 77, 83
Smith, Mallex 40
Strickland, Hunter 57
Suzuki, Ichiro 69
Swanson, Erik 78, 87
Swarzak, Anthony 60
Thompson-Williams, Dom 79
Tuivailala, Sam 81
Vogelbach, Dan 42
Walton, Donnie 79
Warren, Art 81
White, Evan 70, 85

Seattle Mariners 2019

Zammarelli, Nick 79

Ballpark diagrams for Baseball Prospectus are created by THIRTY81Project, a design concept offering original ballpark artwork, including the new 'Ballparks of 2019' 11 x 17 color print.

Visit **www.thirty81project.com** for full details.

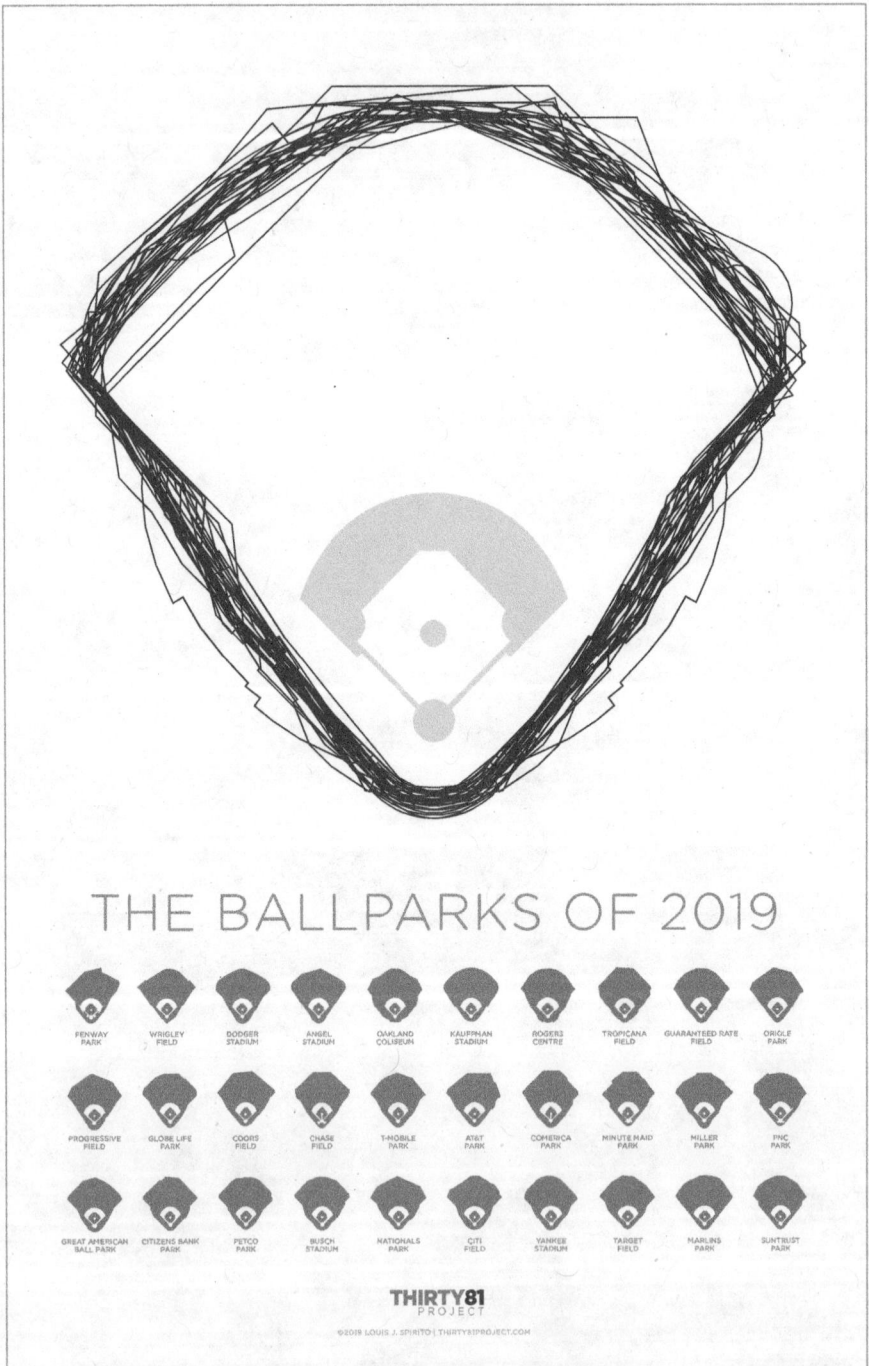